Life Before Genesis

ERRATA

p.12, 1.31 & p.179, 1.7 Should read: <u>The Jesuits in North
America</u> (NOT <u>The Jesuits of North America</u>)
p.13, 1.22 & p.179, 1.11 Should read: Brethren (NOT Bretheren)
p.18, 1.20 Should read: defecate (NOT defacate)
p.25, 1.1 Should read: depredations (NOT depradations)
p.36, 1.34; p.37, 1.10 & p.38, 1.31 Should read: potlatch (NOT
potlach)
p.37, 1.1 Should read: privileges (NOT priviledges)
p.44, 1.21 Should read: palisades (NOT pallisades)
p.54, 1.14 Should read: translucent (NOT transluscent)
p.162, 1.5 Should read: implications (NOT implictions)
p.170, 1.26 Should read: Canterbury (NOT Cantebury)

Toronto Studies in Religion

Edited by

Donald Wiebe
Trinity College
University of Toronto

Vol. 1

PETER LANG
New York · Berne · Frankfurt am Main

David H. Turner

Life Before Genesis

A Conclusion

An Understanding of the Significance of Australian Aboriginal Culture

PETER LANG

New York · Berne · Frankfurt am Main

Library of Congress Cataloging in Publication Data

Turner, David H.
Life Before Genesis: A Conclusion.
(Toronto Studies in Religion; vol. 1)
Bibliography: p.
1. Australian Aborigines - Social Conditions.
2. Australian Aborigines - Politics and Government.
3. Indians of North America - Canada - Social Conditions.
4. Society, Primitive - History.
5. Government, Primitive - History.
6. Stone Age - Australia.
7. Bible.
O.T. Genesis - Miscellanea. I. Title. II. Series.
GN666.T89 1985 306'.0899915 85-7030
ISBN 0-8204-0244-3
ISSN 8756-7385

CIP-Kurztitelaufnahme der Deutschen Bibliothek

Turner, David H.:
Life Before Genesis: A Conclusion: An Understanding of the Significance of Australian Aborig. Culture
/ David H. Turner. — New York; Berne; Frankfurt am Main: Lang, 1985.
    (Toronto Studies in Religion; Vol. 1)
    ISBN 0-8204-0244-3
NE: GT

© Peter Lang Publishing, Inc., New York 1985

Printed by Lang Druck Inc., Liebefeld/Berne (Switzerland)

Toronto Studies in Religion is a new book series concerned essentially with the empirical, analytical, and theoretical study of religion. It aims to publish original research in the historical, phenomenological, and social scientific study of the world's religious traditions as well as new structural and theoretical interpretations of religion in general Philosophical and even speculative approaches to understanding religious phenomena, carried within a generally empirical framework, are welcome. The series will undertake translations of works that deserve a wider readership and that will encourage international scholarly debate. Comprehensive bibliographical studies, original dissertations, symposia, and other appropriate projects will be given consideration.

David Turner's Life Before Genesis: a conclusion (an understanding of the significance of Australian Aboriginal culture) provides a sparkling introduction to the series because it is a comparative work that combines empirical, theoretical and speculative approaches and focuses them on an analysis of a religious text, the Book of Genesis. The basis of Turner's interpretation, as the subtitle indicates, is Australian aboriginal culture, a culture that has also intrigued such scholars as Fraser, Durkheim, Freud, Lévi-Strauss and Mircea Eliade, to mention but a few. His argument, however, draws on Lévi-Strauss' thought, though going well beyond his analysis.

Having elected to remain Stone Age in technology, the Aborigines have, nevertheless, according to Turner, become a 'scientific' people who have achieved that which eludes modern society - peace, order and good government.

Turner's conclusion is founded on more than a decade of ethnological work and numerous publications in the field. His argument is based on comparative analysis of myth and social organization in Australia and Canada and their interpretation along new theoretical lines. It may not be the 'hidden meaning' of the 'text' that is at issue in myth analysis, suggests Turner, but rather its 'hidden context'. He sees that 'hidden context' as a silence within the text - a deafening silence that would preclude ever understanding it or the community that gave it birth. In locating the 'hidden context' of Australian myth Turner finds he has shattered the silence of the <u>Book of Genesis</u>.

Donald Wiebe

To the Memory of
Galiawa

Acknowledgements

This book owes its existence to the enthusiastic skepticism of Don Wiebe.

Publication was facilitated by a grant from the Strehlow Research Foundation, Adelaide, Australia. I am also grateful for the financial assistance of Trinity College and the Centre for Religious Studies, University of Toronto.

I would like to thank RIK Davidson of the University of Toronto Press for encouraging me to persist with this project and Wanda Barrett of the Department of Anthropology, and Kartini Rivers for their secretarial assistance. Dénis Arcand of Perth kindly provided the illustrations. Figure 1, "The Hunter and his Prey", is redrawn with the kind permission of the artist, Clemence Wescoupe.

The Netherlands Institute for Advanced Studies provided me with a year free from teaching and administrative duties at the University of Toronto in 1980-81 which allowed me to consolidate my work in one field and branch into another. This book represents the first fruit of that year.

My friends David Joycey, then the United Church Minister at Elmsley-Lombardy Pastoral Charge near Perth where I live when not in Toronto, and Roger McDonnell, itinerant anthropologist, will know the influence they represent.

As always my wife Ruth saw me through the project and, with my family, lent support in ways only they can know and appreciate.

David H. Turner,
Department of Anthropology
and Trinity College,
University of Toronto,
September, 1984.

Table of Contents

Figures

INTRODUCTION

What could it mean to title a book <u>Life Before Genesis</u>? How can something exist before "the beginning?" What I mean by this is two things: first, I am referring to the beginnings of an historical tradition which has been preceded by another; second, I am referring to the hypothetical circumstances surrounding creation of the first <u>Book of Genesis</u> in the Bible (the second <u>Book of Genesis</u> is to my way of thinking the <u>Gospel According to St. John</u>, but that is another inquiry). In both cases I am referring to a peaceful tradition being overtaken by a destructive tradition. The first <u>Book of Genesis</u> seems to me to preserve the outlines of the first-mentioned tradition and to reflect on its fall into destruction.

What I wish to do here is define the terms of these two, often <u>co-existent</u>, traditions and establish the theoretical relationship between them, bringing to bear the results of 15 years' research on hunting and gathering societies in the process.

Contrary to both popular opinion and professional practice I am not here equating the peaceful tradition with features like communalism, co-operation, sharing. Indeed, as I will show these are in some ways aspects of the <u>destructive</u> tradition in question insofar as they are the outgrowth of an incorporative mechanism that in uniting some, divides them from others. In the societies of the Algonkian Indians of northern Canada we find a prototype for this line of development.

The peaceful tradition, on the other hand, I associate with a formal, institutionalized system of separations into interdependence. It is a tradition always potential but rarely realized in any human society. In fact the only instance I know of where it emerged full blown was amongst the Australian Aborigines at a so-called "Stone Age" level of technological development. There, for reasons which remain a mystery, the accomplishment consolidated and persisted at least long enough for it to be recorded.

i

I say a 'mystery' because being abstract rather than concrete, peaceful rather than warlike (as in conquest and extermination) fragmented rather than unified, withdrawing rather than attacking, the accomplishment is always vulnerable to attack, not only from outside itself but also from forces subordinated within.

It is perhaps indicative of the tradition we ourselves are heir to that we have never seen the Australians for what they really are. Indeed we have situated them at the very bottom rung of the ladder of human evolution. We have deplored their treatment at the hands of Europeans, lamented their present circumstances, pleaded eloquently for their preservation -- but, their preservation as people, not as a culture. Apart from a vacuous cultural relativism which decrees all cultures to be equally valid as 'adaptations' to environmental and social circumstances, no intellectual paradigm we possess can muster a legitimate defence on their behalf. The best we have done is Burridge who, in his Encountering Aborigines, concludes that Aboriginal cultures do not fit evolutionary theories, remain peculiar to themselves, and await the day when an adequate theoretical understanding will materialize.

I recently had the opportunity to review two books on the Australian Aborigines for the Journal Pacific Affairs (56/3). Both sincerely identified with the Aboriginal cause. Both illustrated the central paradox of 'lib/left' 'appreciations' of Australian Aboriginal, or for that matter any other 'pre-capitalist/ industrial', society. While deploring their treatment and present circumstances the authors insisted on locating the objects of their concern at the tail-end of their own civilization's history. The Aborigines, the authors said, were organized by families into domestic groups into exogamous, out-marrying, bands, into regional tribes. The scenario beyond is familiar to us all: chiefdoms, nations, states.

As I said, the reader may be forgiven for being somewhat sceptical of calls to defend Aboriginal culture from such sources when that culture appears to be little more than narrow-minded tribalism.

Other anthropologists point out the exceptional nature of the Autralians from the point of view of theory, the confusion that reigns in the literature on points of description, then blithly conclude that once all this confusion is cleared up the Australians will turn out to be just like any other hunting and gathering people except for some complex ideological elaborations. As Marvin Harris puts it in his Culture, Man and Nature, "kinship ideologies may help to organize an adaptive form of domestic life without accurately or closely reflecting what is actually happening on the ground." On the ground, he says, "like most hunters and gatherers, the Arunta and other Australian aborigines live in composite, bilocal bands."

Admittedly these 'appreciations' are an improvement on 19th century views. Even such prominent spokesmen for Aboriginal rights as Spencer and Gillen -- themselves claiming status as ethnographers -- regarded the Aboriginal languages they heard as so much 'babble' and decreed that they could not translate the myths and songs of the people they studied since they were unintelligible to the natives themselves.

Even the man who has done most to dispel these notions and restore dignity to the Aranda people amongst whom Spencer and Gillin worked, namely the late T.G.H. Strehlow, himself found it necessary to draw analogies between Aboriginal song and poetry and that of the ancient Greeks and old English to substantiate his claims. And yet nowhere is the portrayal of Aboriginal culture more 'in and of itself' than in Strehlow's work.

In Journey to Horseshoe Bend, Strehlow's brilliant account of his father's last days in Central Australia where he had been missionary to the Aranda for 28 years, the European and Aboriginal landscapes are blended so as to be barely distinguishable -- as they are in Aboriginal thought:

iii

The Finke constituted the last link with his lost
boyhood home. It was the ancient Lira Beinta, the
greatest of all sleeping Aranda rivers, famed and
celebrated in the mythology of the Western and
Southern Aranda regions. It came down from the
distant MacDonnell Ranges, from the vast rocky
slopes of Rutjubma and Ltarkalibaka: it swept past
Ntarea to the very base of the red mountain mass of
Lalkintinerama; and it rushed from there into its
thirty-five mile gorge south of Hermannsberg, on
its winding way to Irbmangkara, Rutjubma, Ltarkalibaka, and Lalkintinerama -- or as they were known
to the white population, Mt. Sonder, Mt. Giles, and
Mt. Hermannsberg: these were the three great moun-
tains that had greeted his eyes at Hermannsburg
every day he could remember; and Ntarea was his own
home -- the birthplace that bestowed upon him his
Aranda citizenship rights which no man could ever
take away from him. The high mountain of Lalkintinerama, over whose red, pine-studded dome the baby
Twins of Ntarea had wandered after leaving their
birthplace in Palm Valley, the two desert oaks in
the sandhills north of Hermannsburg which indicated
the furthest point of their wanderings, the second
pair of desert oaks on the southern bank of the
Finke which marked the place where they had paused
before diving into the deep pool of Ntarea, the
rounded hill of Alkumbadora which had come into
being when the frantic mother of the twins threw
away her pitchi upon seeing the foam flakes rising
on the disturbed waters of Ntarea after her babies
had leapt into it: all these sites were familiar
to Theo, and the traditions connected with them
were his birthright, though so far he knew the myth
only in its barest outline and had not yet heard
the sacred verses.

'Theo' is Ted Strehlow, born, raised and buried amongst the
Aranda and here accompanying his father on his last journey to
Horseshoe Bend and 'civilization' in a vain attempt to save his
life. None of the rest of us have had Ted Strehlow's advantage,
hence his fluency -- and it shows. But Anthropologists had
'theory' and Ted Strehlow did not. And that showed too. He
ended life an isolated, lonely, bitter man. All he had were the
Aranda.

iv

The Australians have, in fact, fared better in recent popular culture than they have at the hands of 'theory'. In, of all places, the film version of Tom Wolfe's book The Right Stuff an episode has been cut in as John Glenn orbits the globe which creates the distinct impression that outerspace is not the only mystery on or off this earth. Fellow astronaut Gordon Cooper arrives at the tracking station at Muchea, Western Australia, to monitor the orbit. Aborigines are hanging about and one of them asks Cooper what they're doing there. Cooper tries to explain and the Aborigine nods: "that old man", he says, pointing to a figure sitting on the rocks nearby, "he knows all about the stars and the milky way". "That's good," replies Cooper, "we can use all the help we can get." As Glenn passes overhead the Aborigines are singing and dancing around an open fire. The sparks fly up into the sky. Glenn suddenly finds his capsule surrounded by a mass of very small particles all brilliantly lit up as if they were luminescent -- like sparks or fireflies. Their source is inexplicable. But the association sees Glenn through some technical malfunctions and safely back into the earth's atmosphere. The Aboriginal sequence, by the way, is not in the book.

In the Australian film The Last Wave, a white lawyer (Richard Chamberlain) becomes entangled with a group of Aborigines in a legal aid case involving the death of one of their numbers. These Aborigines are the last of the line of people who originally owned and occupied the Sydney area where the film is set. They and their forbears have been religiously handing down the story of and ritual associated with a second wave which, legend says, will come again to destroy the earth. Chamberlain's mother's grandfather was apparently Aboriginal. He becomes the agent of Dreamtime beings called Mulku in fulfilling the prophecy.

Certainly the film dwells on the supposed extraordinary psychic powers of Aborigines -- their ability to communicate through telepathy and their use of sorcery (in a society so rule-governed with people so close together it is little wonder they know each other's movements implicitly even when apart; and sorcery is certainly effective on those who believe in it). But the film also portrays these Aborigines as people who, above all else, value 'the law'.

The film, by the way, stars two of my Nawarga from Groote Eylandt, Morris and Cedric Lalara; one of my Na:niganggwa, Roy Bara; and two of my Na:barga, Nandjiwarra and Walter Amagula (to translate these terms of reference into 'kinship' terms would be to denigrate Aboriginal culture; their real meanings will become apparent later).

I was on Groote Eylandt in Arnhem Land, when Neil Armstrong set foot on the moon, July 20, 1969. I was sitting with Old Galiawa and a radio was on beside us monitoring the event. Galiawa asked what was happening. I told him a man was landing on the moon. He looked up in the sky and said,

"Any tucker there?"

"No", I replied.

"Any water?"

"None of that either."

"Rubbish place," he said knowingly and went back to the business of carving his spear. A man ahead of his time.

Counterpoised to the Australians are the Algonkians of Canada -- alternately competitive and cooperative each in their own incorporating whole, aggressive against outsiders, dynamic within, all in the interests of achieving self-sufficiency within their not so mutually-respected ranges.

The Algonkians are, or rather were in the pre-contact period, the very prototype of progressive,in-the-technological-sense, history. Theirs was the band/stone age, tribe-chiefdom/basic metals, State/industrialization zig-zag of 'evolutionary' human development.

vi

And yet these two traditions, the Algonkians' and the Australians', did not exist in isolation. In a world of competitive/cooperative wholes some, perhaps the weaker amongst them, seek a confederative course, at least amongst themselves. Others simply withdraw into splendid isolation or peaceful subordination.

Indeed, even within the same tradition, the same society, the same individual, the two trends -- incorporation and confederation -- may reveal themselves in shifting emphasis as circumstances alter and new opportunities present themselves.

What I am in fact describing here is the very stuff of which not only my anthropology but the Book of Genesis is made. I may not encompass all the facts available. Confirmation may even have to await the appearance of new facts yet to be discovered. But I think that what I describe here is sufficiently well-documented to make the implications I draw at least interesting. And that, perhaps, is enough. For if my ethnography is sound and if history works the way I think it does then the first Book of Genesis makes sense as an historical document. Not perhaps as literally historical (some might say 'hysterical') as the Creationists would have it: but then not nearly so mythological as the Symbolists and Scientists would have it either.

The organization of the book reflects the idea it contains: within the 'fallen' world of the Algonkians we begin to see glimpses of 'redemption'. The signs then become more apparent amongst the Pacific West Coast peoples of Canada. From here we leap across the Pacific to encounter these 'redemptive' features full-blown amongst the Aborigines of northern Australia. Then we make our way to the interior to see the precursor (?) of this development (its 'fallen' state?) before moving to an explanation and on to Palestine where a similar process seems to have occurred -- if Genesis is to be believed!

INCORPORATION

Figure 1. The Hunter and his Prey, Clemence Wescoupe

CREE

While working in Australia between 1969 and 1974 (I went back for the first time only this year) it occurred to me that somewhere there must be a hunting and gathering society that was all that the Australians were not. Indeed the Groote Eylandters themselves imagined such a possibility in their myths (one of which I will recount later).

What seemed to be at issue was a society based more on pragmatism than prescription, on co-production as a basis for association than proprietary jurisdiction, on inclusive wholes than on federated parts. A survey of the Canadian northern Algonkian literature indicated such a possibility there. In particular I was struck with Dunning's work on the northern Ojibwa which seemed to suggest certain Australian features such as totems and clans emerging out of a northern Algonkian or Cree base. In fact Dunning, in contrast to his colleagues working on Cree, was suggesting that the base in question operated through group as well as individual relationships in terms of a binary division into non-marriageable 'relations' and marriageable 'non-relations'. This distinction, in turn, seemed to rest less on 'kinship' factors and more on co-production association.

Out of this encounter emerged my Algonkian research with Paul Wertman, then an M.A. student at the University of Manitoba.

As it turned out, the northern Algonkians proved somewhat less than all that the Australians were not, but somewhat more than other researchers had suspected.

I have characterized Cree society as 'locality-incorporative/production group unity'. People in such societies live according to the formula, $1 + 1 = 1$.

Here, many are continually merging into one, conceptually speaking. For instance in the domain of kinship and marriage, a man and a woman marry and become 'parents', call their offspring 'our children' and refer to them by the same 'kinship' terms. Amongst the Cree, for example, the father and mother call their son, Nikosis, their daughter nitanis. Their children call their father Nipapa and their mother nimama in turn. If this sounds familiar, it should because it's precisely the way we do it too. Only we take it all one step further and merge the woman into the legal person of the man on marriage. Until very recently, almost everywhere, her property became his, his surname hers. The Cree have adopted our surname system but were never so chauvinist as this.

Societies such as the Cree's are 'locality' based in the sense that working relationships flow from people coming together in space, first in the context of the domestic group and then through the working relationships established by their parents and finally through their own marriages. A boy grows up hunting with his father and his brothers, a girl gathering with her mother and sisters. The boy now comes to meet the sons of the men with whom his father hunts, the girl the daughters of the women with whom her mother gathers, and works with them in turn. After marriage, a young man meets the husband of his wife's sister, a young woman the wife of her husband's brother, and so on. And as they meet and work together they become part of a larger incorporating whole, referring to one another by the same 'kinship' terms. In Cree, Niwicikiwensi is 'blood brother'; Nistes refers to elder males in the brotherhood, Nisim younger males; nimis refers to elder females in the sisterhood, nisim younger females. People outside the brother/sisterhood are called by different terms from those within and alone are eligible for marriage. In other words, marriage is with people outside the range of your own, your workmates', or your workmates' childrens' working relationships. Marriage transforms these 'outsiders' into 'insiders', thereby rendering them ineligible for marriage in the succeeding generation. This process of reaching out to people with whom you do not co-produce continues until the geographical limits of the band are reached -- that is, until it is practically impossible to form and maintain a working relationship because of the geographical distance involved. Then you begin marrying the descendants of people whose working connections within the band have since lapsed.

The 'band', then, is simply the range of active and potentially possible working relationships.

In a locality-incorporative society people are divided first, united second, as a marriage transforms them from nonworkmate to workmates. Beyond the limits of this process they are opposed - as 'us'/'potentially us' to 'them'.

It is predictable then that a person's personal likes and dislikes should change as he or she grows up and marries. Amongst the Shamattawa Cree, brothers and sisters feel close to one another before they marry but begin to grow distant from each other thereafter. Marriage, of course, has drawn them into a different 'corporation' which demands their primary allegiances. Similarly, prospective husbands and wives exhibit restraint and distance before marriage but affection thereafter. Before marriage they are members of 'opposed' insider-outsider groupings. Parents and children, brothers, sisters, by contrast, remain consistently close through their respective lifetimes. People outside the band are, and remain, at best 'strangers', at worst, 'enemies'.

What incorporation as a process does is form people into stable, cohesive work groups by minimizing the presence of aliens through translating them from 'outsiders' into 'insiders'. Each person is thereby provided with a pool of compatible workmates from which he or she can select partners. This particular adaptive strategy would seem oriented more to maximizing the effectiveness of each hunting and foraging group than to maintaining stable relations between them, which is perhaps why the band as a whole is in need of leaders or chiefs. Or, as one Cree hunter at Shamattawa put it:

> The Chief told people where to trap. Before Indian Affairs began building houses the chief would tell people where to live and who they should live with even when people lived in log cabins.

Leaders are there to regulate the independence that exists 'on the ground' both on an individual-to-individual and co-production group-to-co-production group basis. As another Shamattawa informant remarked:

> The best hunter is the most independent and respectable man -- he is looked upon as the father of the family -- is permitted to regulate domestic concerns and determines the route they must take in their hunting excursions.

Leaders are there to move people around the band range and prevent people from 'settling down':

> People trapped in different places after they got married. If they didn't there would be too many people (in one place).

Leaders are there to prevent some people from monopolizing particularly abundant resource areas, leaving others to 'starve':

> They were about 10 in my family with my mother and father and we really had a hard time. We almost starved because we didn't have anything to eat. It was around Kaskattamagin. My father was starving and he had to crawl because he didn't have anything to eat. He fell down because he couldn't stay on his feet. They stayed there about a night. It was cold and in the winter time and my father couldn't find anything to kill. My father managed to kill one prairie chicken and everyone in the family ate it.

The problem -- paradoxically, also the strength of the system -- is that everyone is looking for the best hunting partnership and marriage arrangement. In theory, the better the partnership the greater the rewards:

> For the parents of a man, a woman has to be a good worker; for a woman's parents a man has to be a good hunter.

The leader is also there to convene the band during the summer season where he reminds them of the fact that their collective security depends on arranging an equitable distribution of resources amongst individual groups and even of partnerships so as to keep the better hunters circulating.

In other words, leaving the choice of partners up to the individual creates competition which can undermine the efforts of the band as a whole to survive in its collective space. The tendency for successful partnerships to continue and monopolize abundant resource areas is counterbalanced by the authority of the leader to regulate the joint interests of the band. But the very fact of authority as such presents a leader with an immense temptation -- use of his powers to attract the most effective producers to himself as partners and wives and so establish his own monopoly position.

We see at work here the classic 'forces and relations of production' contradiction so central to Marxist analysis, and hence, the grounds for the emergence of class. For hunters and gatherers in a locality-incorporative society, the level of technological development is insufficient to benefit all members of the band equally under conditions of severe population and re-source variation. When the choice is between virtually nothing for all and self-sufficiency for some, ability and authority may emerge to lay disporportionate claim to scarce resources.

Paradoxically, the more successful the band is in exploiting its range of resources, the more likely it is that these tensions will arise. For in a locality-incorporative society more food means a larger population and a larger population, in turn, needs more food. This means internal conflict, external conflict or the unlikelihood of technological innovation.

It would seem that locality-incorporative peoples anticipated this problem and took steps to delay its emergence. In comparison with the Australians, for instance, the Algonkians generally spaced smaller numbers of people over a wider range of resources in what looks like an effort to remain self-sufficient within certain bounds, given considerable variation in environmental and social conditions. They ranged in bands of from 100 to 200 people over areas of 10,000 to 20,000 square miles. The Shamattawa band's range, for example, contained a wide variety of resources (see Table 1).

Nevertheless, despite this spacing process, crises did occur. At York Factory, for instance, the Hudson's Bay Company records of 1716 report large numbers of 'hunger starved Indians' around the post. In 1879 they again note,

> There was not the dinner by the Indians, which they have now given annually for three years owing to the almost total absence of deer, partridge, etc.

The Indians, the records say, "left the coast and area around the fort and gone to interior."

But by now these crises in resources were by no means unrelated to the presence of the Europeans in the area. In the month of March, 1873, for instance, a permanent staff of twenty two Europeans and nine native servants and apprentices at York Factory, supplemented by no more than 50 transient employees, took in 2,000 partridge, over 12,000 pounds of venison and 173 fish from the surrounding area. But this would have been only an extreme example of what these Indians would have experienced from time to time under traditional conditions.

We can see that in locality-incorporative society there is an in-built pressure for technological change -- a means of remaining within the bounds of one's social relations and natural resources as population expands or resources narrow. The Marxist formula identifies this tendency precisely -- it places technological change at the forefront of history to be accelerated or arrested by a particular form of the social relations of production.

Table 1. Resources in the Shamattawa

Band Range, 1975

Birds

prairie chicken
sharp-tailed grouse
spruce grouse
long tailed grouse
ptarmigan
greater snow goose
blue goose
Canada goose
lesser snow goose
brown goose (white fronted?)
niskisis inowosco (goose)
kankikeoso kekatmitoni
mallard duck
pin tail duck
buffle head duck
canvas-back duck
merganser duck
grebe duck
green winged teal
scoter
popiston
loon
swan
crane
pelican
blue heron
spoonbill
sandpiper
seagull
coot
snipe cock
woodcock
killdeer
tern

Fish

jackfish (pike)   sucker
whitefish   bass
speckled trout   perch
lake trout   catfish
pickerel   tulerbee
sturgeon   maria
lamprey   herring

Mammals

beaver
muskrat
squirrel
rabbit
moose
woodland caribou
barren ground caribou
black bear
polar bear
otter
mink
marten
fisher
lynx
woodchuck
seal
whale
walrus
coyote
mouse
artic fox
cross fox
blue fox
wolf
wolverine

Plants

gooseberries
blueberries
mossberries
strawberries
glockenberries
raspberries
niskimina berries   )
askimina berries   )medicinal
muskegomina berries)properties
nosomina berries   )
osigwapamina berries)

Nevertheless, technological change is difficult at any particular moment in time, and despite the precautions taken by
Indians to minimize the risk of ecological and demographic crises, they did occur to force people off their lands and onto
those of others organized on a similar basis. And therein lies
the problem: for these others too are incorporative bands and
attempting self-sufficiency within their own ranges. Under the
circumstances, then, it is not surprising that warfare was endemic to the way of life.

The early contact period in Canada is replete with records
of out-migration and large scale aggression as bands sought to
usurp each other's positions and territories. All contact with
Europeans did was provide the Indian with a more efficient means
of incorporating and annihilating the other -- steel knives and
guns -- and a new reason for doing so -- the fur trade, participation in which could provide a new kind of self-sufficiency, at
least in relation to other bands. The consequences for some were
devastating.

No sooner had the Algonkians acquired some of the new
technological means of destruction from the French in the 16th
century than they drove the more sedentary Iroquois -- gardeners
not hunters like themselves -- from their corn fields around what
is now Montreal and down into New York State. And when the
Iroquois finally achieved parity they retaliated, not only
against their enemies the Algonkians but also against their
allies the Huron. The incongruity here was that the Huron were
compatriots of the Iroquois in mode of production, language and
kinship. But the Iroquois coveted the Huron's lands along the
fertile shores of Georgian Bay and their middle-man position in
the fur trade.

A single passage from Francis Parkman's Jesuits of North
America captures the terrible beauty of this era of Canadian
history:

In the damp and freshness of a midsummer morning,
when the sun had not yet risen, but when the river
and the sky were red with the glory of approaching
day, the inmates of the fort at Three Rivers were
roused by a tumult of joyous and exultant voices.
They thronged to the shore, priest, soldiers, traders, and officers, mingled with warriors and
shrill-voiced squaws from Huron and Algonkian camps
in the neighbouring forest. Close at hand they saw
twelve or fifteen canoes slowly drifting down the
current of the St. Lawrence, manned by eighty young
Indians, all singing their songs of victory, and
striking their paddles against the edges of their
bark vessels in cadence with their voices. Among
them three Iroquois prisoners stood upright, singing loud and defiantly, as men not fearing torture
or death.

In 1648 came the final assault on the Huron fortress and its
unfortunate 'guests' the Jesuit priests. Amongst them was the
great Brébeuf, called by the Iroquois, Echon. The scene is
vividly reconstructed by E.J. Pratt in his epic poem, Brébeuf and
his Bretheren:

By noon St. Ignace! The arrival there
The signal for the battle-cries of triumph,
The gauntlet of the clubs. The stakes were set
And the ordeal of Joques was re-enacted
Upon the priests -- even with wilder fury,
For here at last was trapped their greatest victim,
Echon. The Iroquois had waited long
For this event. Their hatred for the French and priests
Was to be vented on this sacrifice,
And to that camp had come apostate Hurons,
United with their foes in common hate
To settle up their reckoning with Echon.

As the fur trade pushed north and west beyond this battle-
ground the more adventurous Algonkians moved with it, exhibiting
much the same toleration for their compatriots as the Iroquois
had for theirs. The Ottawas, for instance, now armed with the
rifle, were able to push the Chippewayans back from the reaches
of York Factory, the Hudson's Bay Company's main trading post on
the Bay, and establish themselves in their place. York Factory
was originally French (est. 1682) but after changing hands a

number of times was finally ceded to the English by the Treaty of
Utrecht in 1713. Subsequent skirmishes between the 'Shumattaway
tribe of the Ottawawa nation' and the Chippeweyans in the area
prompted the Hudson's Bay Company to issue an edict to their Cree
allies in the interests of maintaining their very considerable
profit margins:

> Send expeditions north to settle at Churchill Ri-
> ver. Instruct Indians not to fight Indians there.
> More trade possible from north than presently have
> at York Factory.

These Indians (not to mention their European allies) were
following the dictates of an ancient and compelling logic:

my band $\Longrightarrow$ your band $\Longrightarrow$ my band over your band

The Indian, as I have said, was enamoured with the possibility of a new technological means of destruction -- after knives
and hatchets, the rifle -- and a new mode of production -- the
fur trade -- as a means to the solution of his locality-incorporative problems.

Involvement in the fur trade heralded a new kind of self-
sufficiency that could literally be bought rather than caught and
then perpetuated through monopoly control as suppliers and
middlemen. A change in social relations appropriate to the new
technology might have occurred but for the fact that the Europeans in turn monopolized the capitalist side of the venture. It
is they, paradoxically, that we have to thank for the persistence
of the locality-incorporative tradition amongst Indian peoples
down to the present day -- that is, amongst those Indian peoples
still alive to practice it after their sojourn with their new
'solution' had come to an end.

Prior to the recent work of Harvey Feit (1983) we thought
that the family hunting territory system which ethnographers had
recorded amongst the Algonkians was contact-induced -- our

attempt to regulate their production of furs. The institution
could therefore be 'subtracted' from ethnographic accounts to
give us a true picture of the traditional situation. Family
hunting territories were patrilineally-inherited jurisdictions
within the band range which vested 'title' in land and resources
in the domestic group. What Harvey Feit has shown, though, is
that the registered trapline aspect of this system -- the part
imposed by EuroCanadians -- was in fact superimposed on traditional jurisdictions concerned with regulating hunting activities
with respect to certain resources such as beaver and moose.

As to why these jurisdictions exist, in my view they were
likely a response to internal divisions and emerging class distinctions in the form of competition for hunting partners, monop-
olization of the best hunting territories, autocratic leaders and
anarchistic followers. The idea of mutually respected 'sover-
eignties' is one that might well have occured to regulate this
conflict. However, amongst the Algonkians they were but weakly
developed and, in fact, hovered tentatively and precariously over
a locality-incorporative base which continued to shape basic
relationships and give definition to relationship terms.

* * * * *

In my locality-incorporative society I worry a great deal
about strangers. I am constantly on the look-out for them as I
search for food lest they encroach on my space and lay claim to
its resources. I know they will define me as 'enemy' in advance
and would kill me before I would kill them. At home I have to be
careful to create a good impression as a worker so that I can
attract the best hunting and marriage partners and thereby live a
better life. And yet I must take care not to become too attached
to one partner lest I find a better one at some later date. At
the same time I must be sufficiently loyal to retain their association when I need it. I resent taking orders from my leaders
which often undermines my independence. I'm also never sure but

that they aren't using their position to further their own interests by selecting out the best hunting areas for themselves and
their friends. But I need their organizing abilities to protect
me from outsiders when the situation arises. And I must admit I
aspire to be leader myself for the same reasons, but how to do so
unless I am seen to be furthering the interests of my fellows?

*   *   *   *   *

These, then, are the individual expressions of the collective concerns that underlie life in locality-incorporative
society: how to resolve authority to freedom? Continuity to
mobility? Pragmatism to stability? Autonomy to security?
These, then, are the kinds of concerns that set the mythological
process in motion.

Iyas

The story of Iyas is one of the Sacred Legends of the Sandy Lake
Cree. The Sandy Lake Cree are a people who survived both other
Indians and Europeans to continue down to the present day. They
live in north-west Ontario near the inlet of the Severen River.

Were we to take the tale of Iyas literally, it would make no
sense. Man conversing with animals? Humans and animals alike
with extraordinary powers to do evil and occasional good in the
world? But once we realize that these 'animals', these 'evil-
doing humans with animal features' are but more or less remote
'others' thrown up by locality-incorporative logic who require
equally extraordinary humans ('we's') to combat them, then the
tale begins to make eminent sense. In fact, equipped with a
general knowledge of locality-incorporative principles and practices and a Lévi-Straussian perspective on mythological thought,
the tales can be read and understood almost intuitively, even by
a White Man. In the Lévi-Straussian perspective, mythological
thought seeks to mask oppositions by creating the illusions of
solutions to problems that are real.

The story of Iyas begins deep in the northern forests near a
great lake where the man Way-mishoos lives with his two wives and
child. The child Iyas, though, is not his own but his elder
wife's by a previous marriage. Iyas is devoted to his mother and
they spend many happy hours together.

Way-mishoos' younger wife is without child and she falls in
love with Iyas. But Iyas rebuffs her amorous advances and she is
so affronted that she plots revenge. One day when Iyas is away
hunting she goes into the forest and scratches herself with the
thorns of a raspberry bush. Then she runs in a frenzy to her
husband crying that Iyas has tried to rape her. Way-mishoos is
so outraged that he lays plans to kill Iyas.

In the context of locality-incorporative society, the union
of Iyas and his step-father's wife would constitute a major regression toward domestic group autonomy -- the self-reproduction

of the family. In theory this would undermine the integrity of
the larger band of which Way-mishoos and his family presumably
form a part. Iyas, then, is right to reject this course. But
Iyas apparent complicity in realizing this extreme with his presumed rape of Way-mishoos' wife, causes his step-father to re-
nounce him. This propels Iyas, paradoxically, in completely the
opposite direction -- toward the outer limits of locality-incorporative society, that is, into another band.

Way-mishoos now invites his step-son to hunt with him on a
lonely island in the great lake where the giant seagulls nest.
But while Iyas is climbing the cliffs in search of their eggs,
Way-mishoos paddles off leaving him to their mercy. He shouts,
"Seagulls! There is a thief at your nest. Destroy him! Destroy
him!"

Thus isolated amongst a hostile band, Way-mishoos is sure he
will be killed. But the chief of the seagulls recognizes Iyas
from his dreams: it is through dreams that guardianship relations are formed. The seagulls spare his life. Iyas then asks
one of the seagulls to carry him out over his step-father's canoe
so that he can defacate on him. But what Iyas intends as a show
of contempt for Way-mishoos is interpreted by his step-father as
evidence of his demise. The stool has the smell of man on it.
Way-mishoos concludes that the seagulls must have already ingest-
ed (i.e., incorporated) Iyas. His step-father did not see Iyas
riding on the gull's back.

The extreme situation posed at the outset of the myth is now
weakened: Iyas' removal from his step-father's family now
precludes its self-reproduction in the next generation. Iyas
presence in the alien 'band' now qualifies their alienness.

While amongst the seagulls Iyas has a dream: He sees a long
road through the forest. At the edge of the road he sees Wa-
quish, the red fox; further along the road he sees an evil
creature with a great huge leg with which he crushes people to
death; then he sees two ropes hanging from the sky with large
hooks on the ends which snatch up an Indian as he passes by; next

he sees a grey-haired cannibalistic witch with a huge dog; then another old woman with three beautiful daughters -- but the women are also cannibals and have teeth on their sexual organs which they use to kill their victims; then appear two old women whose eyelids have grown over and from whose elbows protrude sharp spikes with which they kill their prey; and finally his mother appears to him sitting outside her lodge crying over his disappearance.

In other words, Iyas dreams of a journey from alienness back to familiarity. His premonition allows him to do something normal Cree do not do -- plan activities far in advance.

But at this point Iyas does not know how he is to make this journey. There seems no escaping from this island and there is very little food here suitable to his own survival. Not even lichen grow on its barren cliffs. But as he laments his fate, a voice calls out to him from the waters:

"Grandson. Grandson."

It is the spirit of his dead grandfather in the guise of the green-horned serpent who has come to carry him back across the lake to safety. Iyas climbs on his back and they set off, but as they move along, a great black cloud looms up behind them. It is Thunderbird. Before grandfather can escape, Thunderbird swoops down and grasps him, throwing Iyas off into the water. He awakens to find himself on the mainland and he knows that his grandfather is dead.

Iyas, then, has successfully escaped the island, bridging the gap between 'my band' and 'their band' by way of a mediator. Appropriately, there is now food instead of famine. The mediator, as a green-horned serpent, is an appropriately anomalous land-water creature and a complement to the also anomalous air-water seagulls (both share a common association with water and occupy uncompetitive niches in nature) who also saved Iyas' life. It is also appropriate that the mediator should be his grandfather -- someone two generations above him and therefore removed from the politics of co-production group formation, the subject of this tale. Lest it seem contradictory that such a close relative should be naturalized to this extent given our theory of classification here, I should point out that grandfather's alienness consists in the fact that he is dead!

With grandfather's death the permanency of this mediation appears unlikely; but Iyas is able to restore his grandfather to life by taking his serpent's skin and hanging it from a tree branch then throwing branch and all into the water. In so doing he combines elements opposed in nature -- solid and liquid -- into the person of his grandfather; precisely the function of mediators in society.

As Iyas' journey proceeds, he spots animal tracks on the shore and follows them to a fox's den, intending to catch and eat the animals he will find there. But the mother fox confronts Iyas in front of her lodge and offers him some food from her cooking pot as a gesture of good will. She tells him that if he can consume it all he will acquire supernatural powers. This he does and now feels strong enough to journey back to his own mother. But the fox, Wa-quish, warns him of the trials ahead and gives him powerful 'medicine' to face them, then accompanies him on the first part of his journey (that is, to the limits of her band range). Together they find plenty of game to eat and sleep well in the forest.

Iyas, then, has himself successfully become mediator and bridged the gap between bands (Wa-quish is fully fox and therefore wholly alien) to gain access to foreign territory and resources. But the partnership is, in fact, anomalous when judged against Cree reality: it is between an unmarried man and a married woman (or at least a 'mother'). It is destined to be abandoned, but only after Wa-quish saves Iyas from a terrible fate.

The pair come across the lodge of the man with the huge leg as Iyas' dream anticipated. (This man is wholly human, if deformed, and therefore less the alien and more akin to Iyas and his band.) The man feigns hospitality in order to entice Iyas

and Wa-quish into his lodge but once there tries to kill Iyas.
As his leg moves over toward the sleeping hero to crush him Wa-
quish, who has remained awake, leaps upon it and bites it, caus-
ing the man to bleed to death. But Iyas, ever the mediator,
restores him to life as a normal human being. Again he has
bridged the gap between bands. Wa-quish's action illustrates the
importance of hunting partnerships in mediating differences in
Cree society. Or, as one of our Shamattawa informants put it:
"Partners help each other out in time of emergency." The lesson
demonstrated, Wa-quish returns to her lair and Iyas continues
alone on his journey.

As prophecized, Iyas next comes upon the two ropes hanging
from the sky. These the sky people use to snare and eat unsuspecting travellers. But Iyas takes out his tree root medicine
and throws it up at the hooks which snag it and drag it up into
the sky. Meanwhile Iyas runs underneath to safety. The sky
people laugh at the way they have been tricked. A stranger has
passed unnoticed through their band territory.

Next Iyas comes upon the sleeping dog belonging to the old
cannibalistic witch. He waves his mink-hide medicine to trick
the dog into barking and then hides while the old witch comes out
to see who is there. Not finding anyone, she beats the dog for
his mistake. When she leaves Iyas steps out of hiding and
marches past the dog who is now too afraid to call out lest he be
tricked again and suffer another beating.

As in the previous episode, conflict between people is
avoided by someone having successfully passed through alien
territory sight unseen.

Iyas journies on and eventually meets the old woman with the
three ill-equipped daughters. But he inserts his stone medicine
into the women's sexual organs thereby breaking their 'jaws'. In
so doing he restores them all to normality. Iyas now forms a
sexual relationship with these women though it does not develop
into a permanent domestic arrangement. This partnership is somewhat less anomalous than that formed with Wa-quish the fox --

they are after all real people and therefore less alien -- but it remains incomplete and unfulfilled by marriage. Iyas leaves to experience his final adventure before returning home.

He comes upon the lodge of the two blind women who invite him to spend the night. He agrees but recalls his dream and suspects trouble. Sure enough, when he awakes the two women are sitting on either side of the door waiting to stab him as he comes out. But Iyas takes out his deerskin cloth and brushes one of the old women with it. She strikes out with her spiked elbows but only succeeds in stabbing her sister seated opposite. Her sister strikes back and they set to killing each other. When it is all over, Iyas cuts the skin from their eyes and the spikes from their elbows and they return to life as normal people. Says Iyas: "This is the way humans should be!" The women reply: "We shall be able to hunt like other Indians." And indeed there is no anomaly: women -- sisters -- should associate with each other as foraging partners. And so they do, appropriately unconnected to Iyas. He has gone to join his mother.

It is worth noting at this point that there is as yet no mention in the myth of the actual solution practiced by the Cree to resolve tensions in inter-individual and inter-group relations, namely same sex hunting and gathering partnerships connected through same-sex links and conjoined through marriage.

Finally Iyas reaches the camp of Way-mishoos to find that his father-in-law has himself moved into a restricted domestic arrangement. He has excluded Iyas' mother from his camp and taken up with his younger wife who has now born him a child. The self-reproduction of the domestic group is again possible. Iyas has returned 'in the nick of time'. Iyas' mother is relegated to sleeping with the dogs and is treated like one -- that is, she has become 'alien' with respect to Way-mishoos 'band'.

The original opposition, 'self-reproducing domestic group'/ 'alien band' has now been substituted by the weaker terms, 'Way-mishoos and wife'/'mother' which allow of a mediator -- Iyas himself.

Another mediator, Chick-a-dee (unanomalous relative to seagull and green serpent) arrives to tell Iyas' mother that her son
is coming. She rushes out to meet him, thereby distancing herself even further from her husband and his deviation. Together,
Iyas and his mother plot their revenge. In theory, the pair must
be killed if self-reproduction of the domestic group is to be
prevented. Predictably, first to go is their child.

Iyas tells his mother to go into Way-mishoos' lodge and
throw their child into the fire. She does and quickly exits with
Way-mishoos in hot pursuit. But when he see Iyas he knows he
doesn't stand a chance. He offers gifts in an effort to effect a
reconciliation but Iyas rejects them contemptuously: reconciliation would only resurrect the original domestic arrangement, itself part of the problem. But Iyas feigns conciliation in order
to lure his step-father into a false sense of security. In fact,
Iyas has a terrible death planned for him.

Iyas tells Way-mishoos that he has dreamed a dream. The
whole world will be consumed by flames and everyone will die because of the wickedness they have created. Then Iyas tells the
animals to flee across the lake so that they will be saved. Next
he clears a circle in the bush where he and his mother can go to
escape the flames. Finally he starts the fire by shooting off
his arrows in four cardinal directions -- that is around the circumference of Way-mishoos' 'band' range. Then he tells Way-
mishoos that the only way he can save himself is to 'dig a hole
in the ground, fill it with grease and get in.' This Way-mishoos
and his wife do. The flames engulf them and the grease causes
them to burn with a fierce intensity. And so the couple die a
painful death -- in their own small self-reproducing space!

But is the problem resolved? Iyas and his mother are now
alone in a barren land. Iyas has solved the problem by eradicat-
ing both the possibility of domestic group autonomy and band
existence. What's more, he himself is now in a potentially self-
reproducing domestic group situation, and inappropriately with

his mother, although without the resources to support themselves. They might move away to take advantage of Iyas' recent
partnerships but for the fact that all of them are in some way
anomalous and therefore unformable.

In the end, the myth admits failure. Mediation by the individual across band lines is merely the _illusion_ of a _resolu-
tion_. The real alternative is the one that is never mentioned in
the tale: marriage and co-production ties transforming outsiders
into insiders within the limits of the band.

Iyas rightly senses that he and his mother 'were no longer
needed in this world.' He transforms himself into a robin, his
mother into a toad. At least in these mutually-exclusive forms
their reproduction as a domestic group will be impossible. Yet
both will be free to follow their own routes to their own partners without infringing on other bands' domains -- Iyas through
the air his mother through water. Their efforts have failed to
combine the uncombinable in any better form than is present in
reality.

Windigo

The Windigo is a Cree cannibal creature whose depradations are recounted in Algonkian mythology. Cannibalism is a superb metaphor for the social process of incorporation: something external is internalized and becomes part of oneself. We have already encountered the metaphor in the Iyas myth in the form of the old cannibalistic witch and the women with the three ill-equipped daughters, all trying to incorporate unsuspecting victims to a degree that represents part of the problem the myth is trying to solve.

Incorporation is appropriate food for thought under extreme environmental conditions when fundamental questions about the social order are being raised. It is perhaps predictable, then, that Windigo creatures should appear in myth under conditions of winter freeze and summer storm when a crisis in resources is most likely.

Most observers, however, would rather see cannibalistic practices in myth as a record of actual behaviour under crisis conditions. This reinforces a prejudice deep inside us that the people who recount these myths are but one step removed from the animal kingdom. But let me reassure the reader: there is no evidence whatsoever of cannibalism amongst northern Algonkians. Not for purposes of acquiring food anyway. Ritual cannibalism, however, did exist. Here, some part of a slain enemy would be consumed in the belief that his valour would be transferred to the consumer. In principle this act was not unlike our Holy Communion where the congregation partakes of the 'flesh and blood' of Christ. In practice, though, the Algonkians did occasionally partake of more than was necessary to make a symbolic point. As Skinner in his Notes on Eastern Cree and Northern Salteaux remarks, "Famous persons, when captured, were sometimes tied to a stake, cut up piecemeal while alive, boiled and eaten before their own eyes. But as Skinner points out, the normal procedure was merely to "eat a piece of fat from the thigh of the slain victim."

In a Cree myth recorded at Shamattawa, a man with Windigo tendencies eats his wife and would have eaten his son but for the fact that the son was living with his grandfather. The man now turns into a full-fledged Windigo and goes in search of more people to eat.

What we have at the outset, then, is movement toward extreme domestic group autonomy as in the Iyas myth, but which is prevented by the son's and grandfather's absence from the father. Objectively, father and son -- any people in adjacent generations are unincorporating. This is because people within each generation must form their own hunting partnerships albeit some of them through ties already established by their parents in the previous level. In the myth, incorporation of grandfather-son by Windigo would preclude the formation of such co-production ties.

Next in the tale, grandfather eats Windigo's son thereby realizing the tension emerging in the first episode in binary terms as one between two adjacent generations. Then a qualifier is introduced to weaken the opposition between them: Atouscan, as the grandfather is called, and the Windigo, his son, come together to stand against 'the people' or outsiders. Whether these are merely outside their own domestic arrangement or outside their band, the myth does not specify. Indeed it is the presence of these two outsiders who seem to force this relationship between the two men. What this seems to be suggesting, then, is that Cree co-production arrangements are not the positive aspect of Cree culture we thought they were but are rather a negative response to a threat from outside. The remainder of the myth, in fact, explores this very possibility.

Atouscan and Windigo now encounter and defeat successive groups of these outsiders. First they come across the tracks of humans which they follow to their camp. They wait until all are in their tents then rush in to 'twist their heads off'. But in

the ensuing struggle the enemy prove too much for the younger
Windigo and they begin to get the better of him. Hearing his son
in danger, Atouscan rushes to his aid and breaks the back of one
of the assailants. Then the two men set about killing and eating
(i.e., incorporating) the rest.

In the absence of a weakening of the insider/outsider opposition at this level to allow a mediator, then, the strong overpower and incorporate the weak. This is an historical rather
than a mythological scenario:

$$\text{my band} \Longrightarrow \text{your band} \Longrightarrow \text{my band over your band.}$$

And the consequences, too, are historical: the two men now hunt
freely in the vicinity.

Atouscan and the Windigo now come across more human tracks
which they again follow to a camp. Here they find the 'caribou
people'. Apart from the implication that these are somewhat more
alien than the previous group, the meaning of the association of
people with caribou is obvious considering the previous episode:
incorporable people=incorporable resources. They fight and the
young boy from the alien camp who might have been a mediator is
instead used as a club by Atouscan to kill all his fellow caribou
people. Then Atouscan and Windigo eat everyone up -- all, that
is, but the young boy's arm. This is perhaps a sign that mediation is still not dead as a possibility -- if only a weakening
of insider/outsider relationships would precede it in the
scenario!

Atouscan and his son now camp together but in separate tents
as opposition once again begins to emerge between them now that
the enemy has been defeated. The Windigo decides to go hunting
and asks Atouscan to watch over his cooking pot lest the Canada
Jays fly down and steal his food. But Atouscan looks in the
cooking pot and sees the 'two hairy parts between a woman's
legs.' He picks them out and eats them, and when his son returns

and finds out what he has done he is furious: "You stole some of my cooking!" he exclaims.

In fact, Atouscan has prevented Windigo from himself incorporating another woman and thereby becoming more self-reproducible than before. At the same time, Windigo's son -- now part and parcel of Atouscan -- has, by ingesting the 'woman', embarked on precisely the same course. The two generations finally stand equal and opposed.

They fight. And just as Atouscan is about to choke his own Windigo son to death, the young man tries to speak. Atouscan releases his grip. "Who will do the killing of 'caribou' for you?" pleads Windigo.

Atouscan releases him and kisses him. From that point on they eat everything they catch.

In other words, each is necessary to the other's success as a hunter both of animals and men. They need one another independently of the presence of a common enemy. Partnerships are a positive aspect of Cree culture not a negative response to a threat from outside as had earlier been hypothesized. Cross-generation relations through which co-production ties of brother/sisterhood are formed are complementary rather than opposed in contrast to the groupings they mediate. This complementarity is partly effected by incorporation of some of those on adjacent generations into the same domestic group.

The degree of incorporation appropriate to the relationship between father and son here is symbolized in the kiss -- a mingling of substance which leaves the independent existence of both parties intact.

In the final analysis the Windigo myth confirms the Cree status quo: the two men are separated on adjacent generations but united in the same domestic group, and complementary insofar as they link otherwise divided co-production groups. Together they are somewhat antagonistic to outsiders defined as those both outside the domestic group and the band.

The Iyas and the Windigo myths, then, are really two sides of the same coin, the first focussing on inter-group, the second on inter-generational, relations. Both confirm the status quo while leaving the basic problem endemic to Cree social structure intact. Both do so through basically the same process, though the Windigo myth barely passes beyond the stage of initial opposition in restating the case for Cree culture. Myth here, after all, as in all societies moved by the same laws as the Cree, is there to convince its audience that they live in the imperfectly best of all possible worlds.

* * * * *

Standing midway between life as lived -- with all its conflicts and contradictions -- and life as thought -- in an effort to minimize the significance of these conflicts and contradictions -- we have encountered the realm of symbolic representation. It is this process that sees social incorporation as cannibalism. In contrast to mythological thought, symbolic thought is metaphoric and therefore devoid of critical commentary. Symbolic thought communicates images, not analyses and arguments. The Windigo figure itself, organs and sinews exposed, dripping ice from its extremities, is such an image. To the artist the image merely seems an appropriate way of communicating a process whose laws remain unfathomable. To us, though, it is rather evidence of the incorporative archetype set in particular historical circumstances which define its particular contents -- here, winter freeze.

Re-examine the Wescoupe print that introduced this Chapter. The man inside the bearskin inside the bear would seem to represent the three levels of incorporation which lie at the very foundation of Cree society -- domestic group, co-production ties established through the previous generation and those established through one's own marriage. The rainbow which bisects this figure reflects in turn the dualism which permeates all aspects of Algonkian life -- male and female, insider/outsider, domestic group/band.

Were I to represent these dimensions, however, I would do so in this manner:

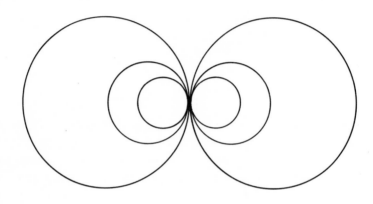

Figure 2.   Analyst's Abstract Representation of Algonkian Social
Relations.

To me, two sets of three concentric circles joined at a common focal point along their circumferences adquately represent the relevant spheres of incorporation extending out through some sex links from ties established within the domestic group of origin and marriage. Is this evidence of the analyst's superior abstacting abilities? I think not. Compare my drawing with the predominant motive behind Algonkian decorative art:

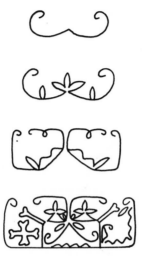

Figure 3. Algonkian Double-Curve Motif (after Speck 1914).

The 'double-curve design', as Speck describes it, consists of
"two opposed incurves as a foundation, with embellishments more
or less elaborate modifying the enclosed space and with variations in the shape and proportions of the whole". The difference between the double-curve design and mine is that theirs
develops mine into an art. And, who knows, perhaps theirs proceeded from theory as much as mine did?
     Algonkian spatial representation follows the same pattern.
In Bringing Home Animals Tanner describes it as based on "a concentric model with the camp space at the centre surrounded by
geographic space, that is the forest and lakes, inhabited by the
animals, at the farthest reaches of which, as well as above and
below, are located various spiritual entities associated with
natural forces". In the 'walking out' ceremony held to mark the
transition in a child's life from 'one who is carried' to 'one

who carries him or herself', the infant is led about a prearrang-
ed space, the boys feigning hunting, the girls collecting, as
they move along. Then they return to their respective same sex
parents with their 'catch'. The double-curve base of that space
is readily apparent:

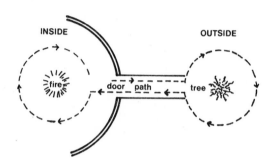

Figure 4.   Spatial Layout of Cree Walking-Out Ceremony (after
             Tanner 1979)

Algonkian totemism reflects locality-incorporative precepts
not so much in the nature of the animal totemized -- all are
appropriately incorporable as edible species -- as in the way the
animal is totemized, that is, on an individual animal to individual person basis. Moreover, the totemic association is effected
through much the same means as one person becomes associated with
another in a hunting-collecting partnership -- through a personal
quest. Likewise, because the association is with the individual
it does not prevent the instigator from 'killing' others of the
species. This emphasis on the individual over the species also
explains why the Algonkians are so fond of keeping pets.

Of course, locality-incorporation is not only a system in
space but a movement in time -- in fact, a lineal movement in

time with progress consisting of technological development and/or
the overthrow and absorption of other peoples. It is not surprising, then, that Algonkians should consider life an irreversable
movement through to death and beyond the stars to the domain of
Manitou and the land of the ancestors. Some ethnographers claim
this vision to have been European-induced. Perhaps. But then
one would still have to explain why European ideas of 'God' and
'Heaven' were readily translatable into Cree and had such an immediate appeal. There is, in fact, some controversy over whether
or not the Algonkians had a notion of one God; but the confusion,
again, is perhaps the anthropologist's. Each incorporating band,
of course, recognized only its own single Creator which led observers of all bands to posit that there were many.

TLINGIT

Amongst the Indians of the Pacific West Coast of Canada we see
the Algonkian idea of hunting territories elaborated into heritable jurisdictions to the point where they can be identified as
clans. The Pacific West Coast tribes range from the Tlingit in
the north to the Chinook in the south. In between are the Haida,
the Tshimshian, the Northern Kwakiutl, the Bella Coola, the Southern Kwakiutl, the Nootka and the Salish. Heritable jurisdictions are more pronounced amongst the northern peoples. The
Tlingit are a case in point.

The Tlingit were divided traditionally into 14 tribes each
settled into villages along the sea coast. Each tribe and village contained representatives of two totemic fraternities --
Raven and Wolf (some argue for a third, Eagle). These two fraternities were in turn subdivided into 20 or so clans, each with
its own totemic emblems. Each village was in theory self-reproducing, containing as it did the representatives of these two
major phratries.

Amongst the Tlingit, as amongst other Pacific West Coast
peoples, the clans as exclusive heritable jurisdictions remained
subordinate to a locality-incorporative feature, the local clan
division. The local clan division consisted of a number of
domestic groups containing people tracing descent matrilineally
from a previous clan member as in a developed clan system, plus
people incorporated through common residence and intermarriage,
the locality-incorporative aspect. And it was the local clan
division not the clan that was the basic land-holding and salient
political unit.

The intersection of lineal and incorporative features is
reflected in the Tlingit's so-called 'kinship' terminology: The
Tlingit distinguish two kinds of people on the parents' generation -- those in father's and those in mother's local clan division, as they would in a fully-developed clan system. Kak and ⅄
at'w refer to men and women respectively in one's own division, sᶜ
m.ɛ and 'ɑ̀tᶜ to men and women in one's father's, with separate

terms distinguishing the mother (ᴸa) and father (is) as individuals. Two kinds of people are also distinguished in one's own
generation -- members of one's father's local clan division and
members of one's own, another developed clan-system feature.

However, in the succeeding generation people are classified
as offspring of marriages not clans: husband and wife both call
their children yit (for males) and si (females). Other people's
children they both call kelk'. This is an incorporative feature:
they are, in effect, 'looking down' at the next generation as
domestic groups -- co-producers -- as in Cree society rather than
as exclusive clans.

In fact, locality-incorporativeness seems actually to en-
close clanness as a principle in Tlingit society much as band
encloses domestic group and even hunting territory in Cree. The
term ᴸilk refers to everyone on the grandparents' generation irrespective of local clan division membership while tšxank' refers
to everyone on the grandchildren's generation. In other words,
'clan' is only being distinguished in the middle generations and
is not an abstract, eternal aspect of the society.

The intersection of lineal and incorporative features is
also reflected in another way which serves to undermine the emergence of clan strictly speaking. People are allowed the choice
of joining the clan division of their mother or the one into
which they moved by marriage. This precludes the emergence of
exclusive lines of clan jurisdiction.

Alongside the underdeveloped clan principle is an underdeveloped federative tendency. Marriage links local clan divisions
into alliance relations but transcends village lines only amongst
the nobility class. Indeed, the presence of class itself is an
indication of the weakness of clan-federation. Economic
exchanges also occur between local clan divisions but the
competitive edge they exhibit belies their definition as a fully
federative force.

The institution of the potlach aims at increasing the pres-
tige and power of one's local clan division by acquiring the

titles, priviledges -- and even hunting territories -- of those of another division. Potlatches are generally held on the death of a chief when his titles become 'vacant' (another indication of the weakness of clan). Indeed, chiefs at all levels had constantly to justify their claims to clan crests and totemic emblems representing their clans by continually out-giving their rivals in this manner. Failure to match or surpass the gifts of a rival meant loss of status and property not only on the part of the individual involved but often for the entire clan segment.

The potlach, though, does have two federative features: it provides for the peaceful -- if competitive -- transfer of territories between people who might otherwise have fought over them; and, during the mortuary rites associated with the chief's death, the chief's clan division and phratry are required to make payment to those in the phratry opposite, the ones actually to perform the ceremony. In fact, the existence of the fraternity itself -- local clan divisions linked into a fraternal alliance through affiliation with a common totemic being -- is itself a federative tendency.

However, as most ethnographers of the Pacific West Coast have observed, the predominant tendency there was 'feudal'. Oberg, in The Social Economy of the Tlingit Indians, points out that amongst the Tlingit "class lines run across the clan and phratry and form a unit probably stronger than the clan itself." Three named hereditary classes were in fact emerging in Pacific West Coast society generally at the time of contact, namely, nobility, commoners and slaves. Only the nobility though had really consolidated its position. It was the nobility, then, who stood poised to seize the clan jurisdiction and supress the federative tendency -- as in relations between clans -- as it emerged and then bend it to the more singular purpose of dominating class rivals and one's 'own' commoners alike.

It is the position of slaves that best illustrates the weakness of the clan-federative tendency and its inability to subordinate locality-incorporative forces: slaves were the members of foreign clan segments captured in war and, despite the presence of common totemic affiliation, they were bound to servitude for the duration of their capture if they were not killed during pot-latching merely to demonstrate the superior wealth of an aspiring chief. Objectively their status was lower than that of the Un-touchables in the Indian caste system: their bodies were used as rollers over which their captors launched their war canoes.

The circumstances under which clan-federation was at least an emerging tendency amongst the Tlingit and other Pacific West Coast peoples were these: The Pacific West Coast Indians were hunters, fishermen and gatherers, not agriculturalists. Yet the ocean provided them with a stable, year-round food supply and permitted large groups of them to live in settled villages scat-tered up and down the coast. However, an important item of their diet, salmon and candlefish, migrated annually up the inland waterways and had to be followed there to be caught. Also in the mountainous interior were bear, deer, and other game. Each tribe required access to these resources but, settled as they were on the coast, they were unable to police the areas they frequented against encroachment by Athabaskan hunters from the east or by their own West Coast neighbours. The contradiction between the forces and relations of production here -- as amongst the Algonkians -- is easy to discern.

Warfare was obviously one response to this problem. Tradi-tion holds that the Haida drove the southern Tlingit off their lands to occupy their present territory; the Kwakiutl say that they originally arrived in the area they now occupy and incorpor-ated an indigenous group there; the Nootka habitually raided and killed their neighbours even in historic times to extend their own holdings.

Clan-federation -- not to mention the potlach -- is the alternative idea that might have eventually occurred.

* * * * *

Considering these two competing tendencies in Pacific West Coast society it is not surprising that we should find two competing logics of thought reflected in their myths. Here the logic of thought which proceeds from a statement of opposition toward the creation of the illusion of a solution encounters, and predictably subordinates, another which begins with a statement of mediation and proceeds (if that is the right word) through the emergence of opposition as mediators are removed. We gained a hint of this logic in the Iyas tale though I did not mention it at the time. The hunting partnership that links Atouscan and Windigo together in precarious alliance is eventually removed to allow the conflict potential between them to rise to the surface. Only a reaffirmation of Cree culture prevents this from happening. And in so doing it justifies the status quo in a manner following from the other logic of thought.

The First War of the World, a Tlingit myth collected by John Swanton, actually seems to contain an explicit statement of the theoretical problem I have deduced as underlying Pacific West Coast society, as undermining the attempts of people there to consolidate the clan principle, namely the problem of over-incorporation.

The time is winter when, in theory, environmental extremes raise fundamental questions about the adequacy of existing living arrangements.

The First War in the World

A man named Xaku⁻tc! is hunting with his brother-in-law and
spears a porpoise near to where a devilfish lives. As they are
skinning it, the blood spills out and spreads over the water.
Xaku'tc! tells his brother-in-law to keep a sharp lookout for the
devilfish. Then they see it coming up towards them from under
the water, arms extended.

It is not clear from the text what happens next: Xaku'tc!
has a spear and his brother-in-law a knife. The tale says the
one with the knife leaped at the devilfish, leaving the 'brother-
in-law' to fend for himself. After a long fight 'he' killed the
devilfish and both men sunk with it, finally resurfacing at a
place called Narrow Point. But when the people there cut open
the devilfish they found only Xaku⁻tc!'s body: 'He it was who
killed the devilfish,' says the tale.

The ambiguity could be merely confusion. However, it could
also be a statement about 'overincorporation'. A brother-in-law
relationship is an incorporative relationship in this type of
society. Actual activation of co-production association would
draw the partners even closer together. In the extreme case they
become one. As one they are killed -- incorporated -- by an
alien band. The myth, then, is not only describing an incorporative social process, it is also evaluating it. Incorporation,
the myth implies, unifies but also divides and destroys. This
interpretation is supported by the commentary which follows next
in the myth.

After his death Xaku⁻tc!'s spirit enters one of his
friends. "In olden times," it is said, "when one killed a great
creature, his strength always came into a certain person,
impelling him to go to war.":

> They used to put a light, thin-skinned coat on this
> person's back to try his strength by endeavouring
> to pull it off, but they were not able to do so.
> They would pull this coat as far back as his shoul-
> ders, but try as hard as they might, they could not
> get it farther. Then (the spirit in this shaman)

told his name. He said, "I am Xaku⁻tcⁱ. I have
been swallowed by a devilfish, and I come to you as
a spirit (yek)." Many people came to see the shaman when he was possessed and to try him with the
coat which no one could pull off. What do you
think it was that held it on his back?

Unable to remove the coat, the incorporative mantle, 'they',
the northerners, start south to war: "They were always warring
with the southern people. They and the southern people hated
each other. When they went down with this shaman (the one with
Xaku⁻tcⁱ's spirit) they always enslaved many women and sometimes
destroyed a whole town, all on account of his strength."

As the tale proceeds a potential mediator appears on the
scene -- a northern boy whom the southerners have captured in
battle. The boy escapes and might have reached his own people
but for the fact that he is recaptured by the southern warrior
Q!oga. However, instead of killing the boy or at least returning
him to his captors as he should have done, Q!oga tells him to
shoot him in the eye with his arrow, which he does. Of course
Q!oga is killed. The myth attributes this turn of events to the
spiritual strength of the northerners. But it appears rather
that Q!oga has thrown off his own incorporative mantle for a
moment to see what might befall. The result is nothing if not
predictable and, in fact, now prevents the young boy from assuming the role of a mediator for the southerners must avenge
Q!oga's death and the northerners can now proceed unhindered into
southern territory in Q!oga's absence. Incorporation is something you can't live with and you can't live without, at least as
long as it is not abandoned by all parties simultaneously.

In other words incorporation, besides being a source of conflict between tribes, is also a weakener which, under normal circumstances, maintains them independently one from the other.
Once this weakener is removed, as Q!oga discovers, opposition
prevails, but even with the weakener in place, opposition prevails. Thought is here proceeding in the direction,

mediation ⟶ weakener (removed) ⟶ opposition,

though introduced by a statement of opposition, a defining feature of the mythologic we encountered as predominant in the Cree myths.

Northerners continue to fight southerners in the tale, fulfilling the my band ——→ your band ===→ my band over your band historical scenario. But each time an attack is made the victorious party, instead of consolidating its hold, returns to its home base unable or unwilling to abandon the actual mobility pattern of Tlingit society -- back and forth to and from coastal and inland haunts.

At this point another potential mediator arises, the young man Murrelet. Murrelet is also captured by the southerners and is allowed to live because of his extraordinary skills which may be of use to them. He has been trained to run up the face of steep cliffs and thereby gain an advantage over his enemies. The southerners wish to see evidence of his abilities so they order him to scale a nearby cliff, apparently oblivious to the obvious fact that if he does so he will escape! He does, flying off above them.

Unperturbed (perhaps they wanted him to escape so as to be rid of a potential mediator!), the southern war party now moves on to a beach where they make camp. Here they tie up Murrelet's steersman, planning to use him for an anchor. Murrelet, however, hears his cries and flies down to rescue him, setting the south-erners' canoes adrift in the process. The steersman is, 'per-haps' his brother says the tale; (but could be his brother-in-law, thereby duplicating the relationship of Xaku⁻tc! and his partner at the outset of the myth). Incorporative ties are renewed and mediation fails to materialize. Indeed, it is as if everyone expects mediation to fail and incorporation to prevail. Again unperturbed, the southerners calmly go about the business of retrieving their canoes, forgetting all about Murrelet and his steersman.

In the absence of a mediator the status quo, predictably, proceeds unabated. The southerners continue north and reach a fort which they raze but spare one 'high caste' woman from death. Unbeknown to her captors the possibility of yet another mediator has now arisen. The woman is pregnant when captured and gives birth to a boy when she arrives in the south. Conceived in the north and raised in the south, he seems ideally placed to mediate relations between the two groups. But the boy grows up ignorant of his mother's slave status. Then one day he sees a young man kick his mother in the nose and realizes the truth. But he asks: "You people know she is my mother. Why don't you take good care of her even if she is a slave?". To him she should be better treated because he, her son, has been raised a southerner.

However, the young man also affirms his northern connection, and he feels the urge to return to his mother's land -- the land of his clan. Mediation, up to now merely potential in his situation, all of a sudden becomes real as a possibility:

> Then he ordered them to make a paddle for him, and they made him a big one. His spirit was so very powerful that he obtained enough blankets for his services to purchase his mother's freedom. Afterwards he got ready to come north with his father (see below) and mother, and they helped him to load his canoe. Before he started his father's people asked him not to bring war upon them.

Just to make sure he does not reincorporate wholly into the northern fold, a southern 'father' has been dispatched to accompany him and his mother on their return journey. Along the way they are careful not to step ashore but anchor instead out in the water, a respect for foreign jurisdiction entirely appropriate to a mediator who is at the same time trying to transcend the problem of incorporation.

The young man is immediately welcomed by his northern 'friends' (presumably those related to him through his mother and northern father as potential hunting partners). The northerners now install him as their war chief and all begin to prepare for an assault on the south. His reincorporation appears complete and mediation doomed to fail: the weakening effect of residence in the south has been removed. But just before his war party

sets off, his southern father reminds the young man to 'remember
the place where he had stayed and not destroy it.' Whether this
mediating function is realized or not we are never told. In all
subsequent encounters related by the tale the incorporative
mantle is securely in place:

> They came straight up to a certain fort without
> attempting to hide, and the fort people shouted,
> 'Come on, you Chilkat people.' They had no iron in
> those days, but were armed with mussel-shell knives
> and spears, and wore rounded wooden fighting hats.
> They destroyed all the men at this fort and en-
> slaved the women and children.

Then the southern people march north in retaliation. They
come upon one fort and destroy it, capturing the women. Then
they move up the inlet and capture a village. But here one of
the women they capture (mother of another potential mediator?)
tricks them into running two canoes down the river at half tide
and the occupants are killed in the rapids. At the next fort
they come to the southerners and destroy all the people there.
But at another they are confronted by men armed with clam shells
who strike them in the face as they try to storm the pallisades.
So they withdraw and move on to another fort where they destroy
everybody. By destroying everybody, of course, including the
women, there is no possibility of mediators arising as before.

By now the southerners think they are getting much the
better of the northern people. Little do they know that 'only a
few were left to look after the forts, most being collected elsewhere'. ('Forts' seem to be an attempt to maintain some kind of
presence in lands you cannot always occupy.)

The southerners' raids continue all summer and everywhere
they go they kill the men and enslave the women and children
(apparently rethinking again the possibility of a mediator!).
Now the southerners come upon one northern fort high on a cliff
occupied by the 'Quarreler' who is so jealous of his wife that he
will let no one live near him. When they stop in front of

his fort he begins to argue with them, castigating them for destructive intentions. The southerners are so distracted by his rhetoric that one of their canoes strikes a rock and splits in two. After rescuing the occupants, the southerners decide that if they remain here much longer the Quarreler will 'quarrel us over as well'. And so they leave.

The anti-incorporative allusions here are too obvious to be missed: one dividing into two; the men saved instead of drowning; the emphasis on dialogue; the Quarreler protecting his 'alliance' relationship with his wife; begrudging respect for the Quarreler's jurisdiction; separation. What seems to be suggested here is a non-human mediator -- abstract culture, clan? -- to stand between incorporating bands, but the possibility is not developed.

Again in the absence of a mediator the southerners now have their 'greatest fight of all'. When it is over the victorious southerners thought that they had destroyed all of the northern people, and that no more raids would be made upon them. But, of course, they are labouring under an illusion. The bulk of the northerners are, in fact, encamped in their coastal villages. And when they learn what has happened, they band together to plot revenge.

The northerners now fashion an enormous canoe out of a single tree, leaving one of its limbs standing upright in the middle. This they sharpen into a stake. Then they head south.

Meanwhile the southerners, thinking they had destroyed all the northerners, are themselves scattered everywhere and do not bother to make forts. They are now easy prey for the northerners, and at the first camp they reach they kill all the men and impale, while yet alive, the women and children on the sharpened limb. They then go about killing people, destroying property, and enslaving women of other camps, so that eventually they kill more of the southern people than the southerners had killed in the north. When they think they have killed everyone they start back for home. But, of course, the northerners hadn't killed everyone. The enemy's weakness was also its strength: many of them, like the northerners before them, were elsewhere at the time though here dispersed over the landscape in locality-incorporative fashion rather than settled down in villages.

In the end, the failure of warfare to solve the problem of alien incursion in the face of mobility to and from villages and within the band range is also admitted: "Since that time (our) people have been freer to camp where they please, and, although the northern and southern people fought each other for a long time ...." So we learn that the southerners did survive after all.

The status quo actually practised in the society finally prevails: warfare and counter-warfare; attempts at incorporating other people and territory; outposts to police remote areas; dispersal over the 'band' range. In its final resignation the myth creates the illusion of a solution and thereby enfolds another logic which has barely proceeded beyond a statement of potential mediation. Here weakeners temporarily holding destructive forces in check were briefly removed, but, without a mediator actually in place, opposition simply overwhelmed the remainder of the tale even to the point of destroying the possibility of mediators, as when alien women and children were put to death along with the men.

And yet, high on a hill, in his fort, safely removed from all that is going on around him, sits the Quarreler and his wife, hinting of yet another possibility -- clan, properly constituted and federated.

*　*　*　*　*

In the art of the Pacific West Coast Indians we also see clearly the interplay of two distinct tendencies, here expressed as symbolic archetypes:

Figure 5.   Painted Box (after Holm, 1965)

The style is termed 'split-representational'.   It is as if a
design has been transferred from a three-dimensional to a one-
dimensional plane. Some take this as sufficient explanation; but
they fail to ask just why such a transfer would have any appeal?
Look more closely at the essential features of this design and
you will see at the base the double curve motif of the northern
Algonkians. But what has happened is that the curves have become
flattened around the circumference to the point of almost being
transformed into rectangular blocks, the significance of which
will become apparent later.   There is some hint of the same
lineal tendency in Algonkian quillwork and beadwork.

We would expect too that religious beliefs would focus less
on the notion of a supreme being and more on a plurality of
deities as clans and phatries emerge within or above incorporating 'bands'.   In fact, ethnographers generally characterize
the beliefs of the Pacific west coast peoples as 'confused', with

but a vaguely developed notion of a single 'God'.   Instead, they
prayed to a 'host of ocean deities on whose good will they relied
for food.'

CONFEDERATION

Figure 6. Central Hill, Gula Lalara

Describing the nature of the land-holding unit (a phrase that is itself indicative of the problem) in Australia proved the most difficult task of my research there. In my Groote Eylandt monograph I employed the term 'local group' to express the Aboriginal reality, stating that this was but a short-form of 'patrilineal local group', meaning that amongst the Warnindilyaugwa and other 'clans' of the area membership in the local group was determined by the father. Or at least most people had the same local group as their father.

Unfortunately the adjective 'patrilineal' here implied something that the Aborigines themselves actually denied -- the existence of a line of descent back to a common ancestor, real or imagined. A more accurate way of putting it would be to say that they found this issue irrelevant. It was enough merely to be a member of the 'local group' as circumscribed in the present by totemic or mythological design.

This, the aspect of unit rather than group, I later tried to encompass in my general work on Australian Aboriginal Social Organization by referring to the 'territorially-defined' land-owning group centred on the continuity of males. Accurate or not it was much too cumbersome a phrase for general use and so I shortened it to 'patri-group'. Again unfortunately, this also conveyed some of the implications I was seeking to avoid. The kinship connotation of the term confounded readers who were also being told that an Aboriginal person was a member of his or her own patri-group while at the same time filiated with their mother's patri-group, their father's mother's and their mother's mother's. I seemed to be saying that a person was filiated with his or her father's patri-group which, however tautological and odd it may sound, was the way it is.

Then after completing a computer simulation of the Groote Eylandt area relationship system I concluded that the territorially-defined land-holding unit was primary over kinship as such in determining interpersonal relationships as defined by so-called kinship terms. This moved me in the direction of even more abstract definitions of the unit in question and away from more 'on-the-ground' translations. This is when I hit upon the idea of 'abstract, eternal jurisdiction' exclusively associated with people through either a) lineal transmission through males or females (the most effective way of achieving exclusivity); b) affiliation with one's 'conception site' or 'birth place'; or c) residence within the jurisdiction in question (the least effective way of achieving exclusivity).

The idea of abstract, eternal jurisdiction is the way I think Aborigines on Groote Eylandt actually conceive of their relation to land apart from its use as a resource; that is, as transluscent cubes enclosing land, sea, air and subterranean space. In short, not as 'land' at all but as Dreamtime substance. This then is what accounts for their religious attachment to the land. Abstract, eternal jurisdiction is an Idea without material foundation (unlike the land itself). Its source must likewise be transcendent.

We can now see how a person might be said to be filiated with his or her father's 'local group' as well as his or her mother's and so on: there really is no kinship in it. It is this that makes use of the term clan so difficult to justify in an Australian Aboriginal context. [1] The term is already associated in the literature with Australian-like jurisdictions emerging out of a co-productive, co-residential, incorporative base where kinship is very much a part of the arrangement. In other words it is associated with situations like those of the Pacific West Coast Indians.

But we do need a short-hand way of referring to the Australian reality -- one that implies transcendence of another, related reality. "Clan", in quotes, is the term I shall use.

I have termed Groote Eylandt Aboriginal society kinline-confederation/production group diversity in type. People in such societies live according to the formula: 1 + 1 = I I. That is, rather than merge into one through mutual association, as the Cree do, people in kinline-confederation society separate into interdependence. The mechanism that achieves this is the exogamous "clan". "Clan" is, as I've said, abstract, eternal jurisdiction over, through and below bounded territory and resources. It is a jurisdiction vested in all men and women of the "clan" differentiated by generation and transmitted lineally. Amongst the Warnindilyangwa transmission is through males but female links would serve equally well. The point is merely to establish a line. Lines can be traced out over reproductive relations in time; in so doing kinship, an aspect of nature, is transformed irrevocably into kinline, an aspect of culture. It is line that makes relations orderly and predictable over generations in time.

On marriage, husband and wife retain their respective "clans" of origin; children become the offspring of but one "parent", the father, considered singly as a member of his "clan". A woman's children are literally those of her 'brother', indeed, of any male in her own "clan" and generation. She is not the mother of the children she bears. These belong exclusively to her husband and his "clan" and generation-mates. Amongst the Warnindilyaugwa, a woman and her "clan"-generation-mates all call the children of the men of her "clan" and generation, Na:nugwa (males) and dadiyawa (females). The woman's own children -- the ones she bears who are really the children of her husband -- they call Naberra (males) and daberra (females). As this implies, despite a sexual division of labour which separates men's from women's work (as in locality-incorporative society) men and women are structurally equivalent within their "clan" compartments. All people of the same "clan" and generation relate to people in all other "clans" and generations in exactly the same way, referring to them by the same terms (with some qualifications I will not go into here).

Procreative beliefs hold the female to be merely a receptacle for release of the procreative force of the male. The male himself is believed to play no physical role in the procreative process. He rather contributes to the spiritual identity of the child, that is, its "clanness". Considering the actual, observed fact that the female bears the child and provides 80% or more of the total diet from her collecting activities (as in all hunter-gatherer societies), it is not surprising that it is the male who should exhibit symptoms of extreme insecurity here. And sure enough, men take themselves up and hide in the bush to perform increase ceremonies designed to ensure the continuation of natural and human species by simulating woman's reproductive processes.

Amongst the Warnindilyaugwa in contrast to the Cree, a person's likes and dislikes are rather more constant throughout his or her lifetime -- as is "clan" affiliation. Brothers and sisters feel close to each other before they marry and continue to do so thereafter. The occasion of their marriage into other "clans" does not affect their own "clan"-of-origin affiliation which continues to hold them. Correspondingly, the restraint and distance that prospective marriage partners feel before marriage continue to characterize their relationship after the alliance is formed.

"Clans" are symbolized totemically, a natural series paralleling a cultural series. For example, two marriageable "clans" may be designated Eaglehawk and Crow -- that is, as complementary (genus of the same type), but opposed (as live meat eater to dead meat eater). On the other hand, two unmarriageable "clans" may be designated East Wind and South-East Wind -- that is, as complementaries distinct and contrasting but not opposed. The metaphor extends even to Aborigine classification of the natural world as such. As Dulcie Levitt writes in Plants and People, her botanical study of Groote Eylandt, "For example, two groups of skinks each of which contains several scientific species, are thought of as brother, and three species of the dragon as sisters."

But if "clans" exclusively associated with a distinct natural species intermarry, one might ask does this not, in fact, contravene the very laws of nature: eagles do not 'marry' crows but other eagles; yet Eagle "clan" marries Crow "clan". There is no contradition, however, for the principle of lineal transmission declares that Eagles only beget other Eagles despite their association with Crows. Crows are merely the receptacle within which Eagles reproduce themselves.

"Clans" that do not regularly intermarry signify their complementary status through association with a common corpus of totemic beings. All affiliate with one common being who traversed (and still traverses in another domain) all their respective "clan" territories, thereby inter-connecting them. To avoid the implication that affiliation with a common denominator incorporates all into one, the linking being itself is usually primarily associated with but one "clan". And, as von Brandenstein, in Names and Substance of the Australian Section System, has observed, even linking beings change 'temperament' as they move from one "clan" country to another.

My own "clan" the Warnungamadada, for instance, owes primary ✗ allegiance to Green Snake while other "clans" in the 'company' as the Aborigines translate it (thereby avoiding the implication that it is a quasi-kinship grouping), owe allegiance to other totems such as Parrot and Central Hill. But it is only Central Hill who traversed all our "clan" estates. Within each "clan" one's own totemic beings also travel about to link each person therein and everyone is named on a particular part of the totem and with particular sites within the estate.

The "clan" system -- the arrangement of "clans" into marriage and company alliances -- has one important advantage over its locality-incorporative rival. It permits the planning of activities in advance of future generations. People come and go, grow or decline in numbers, but "clan" jurisdiction remains eternally vested in the lineal descendents of the present generation. With them you can arrange the future. Rules set down particular patterns of clan alliance which must be followed, past, present and future. These are reflected in people's identities: The <u>Nawarga</u> I mentioned in the Introduction, for instance, are -- or should be -- men in my own "clan" whose mother's are in my mother's "clan"; my <u>Na:niganggwa</u>, men in my mother's "clan" whose mothers are in my father's mother's "clan"; and my <u>Na:barga</u>, men in my mother's "clan" whose mothers are in my mother's mother's "clan". (On Groote Eylandt the ideal is to marry the same "clan" every second generation.) People, culture and nature being what they are, though, it is sometimes difficult to maintain this pattern of alliances -- politics enters in and sometimes population shifts are extreme. But the Warnindilyaugwa and other Australians try. This is partly because, in Australia, economic arrangements follow from these jurisdictional arrangements rather than the other way around, as amongst the Cree.

⤲ The great gatherings of the "clans" to celebrate the activities of the totemic beings who animate them and link them into companies are the occasion for exchanging goods and services across jurisdictional boundaries, particularly items that cannot be obtained locally.

Marriage, by contrast, sets in motion a movement of people across "clan" boundaries in co-production groups composed of a man, his wife and children and perhaps his "clan" brothers or her "clan" sisters, their wives husbands and children. Because each person retains his or her "clan" of origin throughout their lifetime, they gravitate back and forth between their respective estates of origin and marriage, hunting and foraging in the process.

The totem -- the abstract symbol of "clan" -- is also not without its economic, confederative, implications: the totemic species associated with the "clan" must not be consumed by "clan" members. Eating it would be a symbol of all that the "clan" is not -- an incorporative unit. On the other hand, the bandicoots that are forbidden to you in this way are by definition available to those you marry, and perhaps also to members of other "clans" in your totemic fraternity -- certainly to those of other totemic fraternities. (Critics may retort that not all totems are edible and therefore the economic theory is invalid, but then I would reply that each clan has at least some edible totems). Totemism in this aspect, then, is perhaps the essence of complementarity or interdependence: a part of one's own jurisdiction reserved for others, of the other's for those of one's own.

At the very foundation of the confederation process is a 'spacing process' which locates "clan" jurisdictions around small numbers of people and a narrow range of resources, at least relative to the situation in locality-incorporative societies. Population densities in Australia range from two to three people per square mile (which some anthropologists say only agriculturalists can afford) to one person per 35 square miles, still well below the lower end of the locality-incorporative range, that is, one person per a hundred or so square miles. And on one remote island area of Australia, I actually found "clan" boundaries drawn around exclusive resources, one encompassing the water supply, another yams, yet another wild apples, such that no "clan" could be economically self-sufficient in all resources. More to the point, each "clan" jurisdiction was of such a size that its boundaries could have encompassed at least two of the three exclusive resources.

Confederation is aided too by the practice of distinguishing ownership from control, first in the context of ceremonial participation, and second in political dealings between "clans". It is on ceremonial occasions where the dangers of commonality loom largest, this being the time for celebration of common totemic affiliation. Separation of ownership from control subverts this possibility. While members of one's own "clan" jurisdiction perform songs and dances associated with their principal totem, members of the other "clan" jurisdictions they have recently married (by definition in other totemic companies) determine the order of

presentation of the performance and stand vigilant on the sidelines watching for mistakes. When they come they are severely
punished -- occasionally by death.

In a secular context, a "clan" must seek the permission of
those with whom it has recently intermarried before it can allow
those with whom it has not, access to its estates. For all
practical purposes this means consulting others on most of the
"clan's" activities. (I myself was barred from visiting one
"clan" country by the distant totem-mates of my mother's "clan"
to whom the estate belonged simply because that "clan" didn't
like the idea of 'anthropologists'.)

Finally, confederation is aided and abetted by another
institution, the 'section'. The section system is widespread
though not universal in Australia. The Groote Eylanders, for
instance, know of it but have chosen to ignore it as somewhat
'redundant'. What the section system does is render the generations interdependent and guards against another singular possibility -- the emergence of generation mates as such! It does
this by combining alternate generations within each "clan" -- and
in theory within all "clans" with which it is totemically linked
-- into a single category, thereby forming two father-son
'couples' of sections. Paradoxically a dash of unity across
generations is introduced to prevent unity within each generation. In the process this prevents the older men with the most
knowledge and therefore the most power from combining with their
counterparts in other "clans" to form a class of potentially
exploitative gerontocrats.

In a base-two "clan" society where the ideal is intermarriage between the same two "clans" every generation there are two
section 'couples'. One couple is within your own "clan" and
company; the other is within the "clan" and company you marry.
In a base-four "clan" society where the ideal is intermarriage
between the same two "clans" in alternate generations, there are
four section 'couples', one for each of the "clans" distinguished
for marriage purposes.

Amongst the classic base-two "clan", four-section/two section-couple, society, the Kariera of north-west Australia, the section couples are named Banaka-Palyeri, Karimera-Burung. Their rules of combination are as follows:

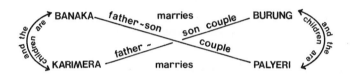

Amongst the classic base- four "clan", eight section/four section/couple, society, the Aranda people of central Australia, the section couples are named,

$$
\begin{array}{lcl}
\text{PANANGKA } (A_1) & - & \text{BANGATA } (A_2) \\
\text{PURULA } (B_1) & - & \text{KAMARA } (B_2) \\
\text{KNGUAREA } (C_1) & - & \text{PALTARA } (C_2) \\
\text{NGALA } (D_1) & - & \text{MBITJANA } (D_2)
\end{array}
$$

Their rules of combination are these:

$$
\begin{array}{lcl}
A_1 & = & B_1 \\
C_1 & = & D_1 \\
B_2 & = & C_2 \\
D_2 & = & A_2
\end{array}
$$

Once instituted, the section system performs two important additional functions. It reinforces marriage alliance rules at the "clan" level and provides a common medium of communication through which relationships to strangers can be quickly and effectively organized. In fact, because of their abstract nature, the sections can be removed from their context in "clan" and manipulated within their own terms to establish rules from which marriage and totemic alliances must proceed. Indeed, the sections may eventually lose touch with the base from which they were originally abstracted and operate to 'merge' the very units whose integrity they were originally designed to protect -- the "clans".

X   Totemism, exogamy, 'spacing', the separation of ownership from control, the section system, the "clan" principle itself -- all are institutional means of 'forcing' people into interdependence by denying them the very possibility of autonomy and self-determination in their various "clan" jurisdictions. Thus is tension transposed from relations between exclusive groups to relations within inclusive groups formed out of alliances between exclusive "clans". Here, in contrast to the locality incorporative situation production groups are diverse not unified. It is this that sets in motion the gravitation of people between their respective estates.

Opposition, then, is thus successfully subordinated to complementarity and the cause of revolutionary upheaval in society vanishes. Instead of confrontation over territory and resources there is accommodation in economic interdependence out of mutual respect for exclusive, abstract, jurisdiction, an exclusiveness that in this context actually promotes peace.

One of the means to this on a practical level is that there is now a mechanism in place for moving people across the landscape in times of ecological or demographic crisis -- that is, to other sectors of the totemic company. At first glance such movements might seem contradictory. A "clan's" jurisdiction is eternal and immutable. How then to accommodate 'outsiders' with their own eternal jurisdictions elsewhere? True, "clans" could not be collapsed into one another to form larger wholes; but the fact of totemic linkage, totemic company, the criss-crossing of totemic tracks through a particular estate, allows a portion of that estate to be affiliated principally with another "clan". The estate thus divided, the jurisdictions can now carry on consistently reproducing their respective totemic identities. It is for this reason that "clan" estates remain 'vacant' long after their owners have departed to establish themselves elsewhere and before they are taken over by other "clans". This gives people time to forget that totemic ties are supposed to remain 'eternal' and immutable.

A case in point is the Warnungwadarbalangwa "clan" of Bickerton Island which migrated to Groote Eylandt over 100 years ago and which today still lays claim to the lands of their origin. This despite their considerable holdings on Groote Eylandt courtesy of their companion "clan" the Warnungwudjaragba there. Over time, the departed "clan" would normally come to be affiliated only with specific sites in its old territory which had been traversed by its principal totemic being. The remainder of the estate could then be claimed by another "clan" with secondary linkages there. But in the Warnungwadarbalangwa case, anthropologists, missionaries and government officials on Groote Eylandt were so intent on an accurate recording of 'tradition' that they assigned the entire "clan" estate on Bickerton Island to the Warnungwadarbalangwa of Groote Eylandt, and recorded it as such on their "clan" maps, much to the delight of the present absentee owners. So did I in my own 1974 monograph on the area.

It has long puzzled anthropologists just how the Australians could have inhabited an entire continent for 30,000 years or more yet find no evidence of organized warfare for territorial acquisition (apart from one exception that proves the rule which I

will come to later) or of extermination of the other. This is
particularly perplexing if we consider that the arts of war were
known even to the Warnindilyaugwa through contacts with the
Macassans, Indonesian traders who reached their northern shores
in search of beche-de-mer (a sea slug traded to the Chinese as a
gourmet's delight), pearl shell and timber. It is not so puzzling once we have discovered the real nature of the Australian's
system of social organization.

Indeed, so sophisticated are the Australians in handling
conflict that they have actually devised means whereby social and
cultural change can proceed from the force of contradiction without impinging on interdependence and social order. This is because these contradictions exist on a strictly intellectual and
experimental plane. This, in turn, is because even such 'competing' social orders as Aranda and Kariera have exactly the same
adaptive advantages.

The basic 'choice' is this: marriage between the same two
"clans" in consecutive generations and two totemic companies
(Kariera) and marriage between the same two "clans" in alternative generations and four totemic companies (Aranda). But no
matter which alternative one chooses the same balance of advantages and disadvantages follows: what one arrangement gains by
way of marriage ties to more "clans" (four in the alternate generation exchange system), it loses by way of totemic ties to
fewer "clans" (one quarter of the "clans" in the universe in the
alternate generation exchange system). The consecutive generation exchange system, by contrast, affords ties to only two
"clans" in the universe by virtue of its separation of that universe into two exclusive totemic companies.

I say 'universe' because a grid of abstract, eternal, exclusive jurisidictions, each of the same type has been superimposed
over all of nature. Each person carries this grid around in his
or her head and brings it to bear in specific situations. Classification of strangers, for instance, is accomplished merely by

locating common points of totemic reference and inserting them into one's own local interpretation of the grid. In the absence of actual totemic correspondences, nature is consulted directly: almost everywhere, the sun, the moon and the stars each belong to someone. If there is still a problem, if people are encountered who are so uncivilized as not to even know what is at issue, their position is fixed in terms of the cardinal points, which these Aborigines also totemize, and a one-way relationship proceeds from this.

The economic gains and losses of one or the other system of "clan" alliances arranged within this grid are these: on the one hand more trading ties and fewer foraging ties where marriage is with the same "clan" in consecutive generations and there are two totemic companies; on the other hand more foraging ties and fewer trading ties where marriage is with the same "clan" in alternate generations and there are four totemic companies. Substituting one system for the other, then, does not result in any gain or loss of adaptive advantage.

On one level there is no doubt but that the two classic orders are contradictory. People in an Aranda-type society, for instance, are prohibited from marrying those whom people in a Kariera society prescribe, namely someone in the mother's "clan". The Aranda also recognize four totemic companies compared to the Kariera's two.

Now suppose these Aranda meet some Kariera-type people at a ceremony who convince them that a mythological being, of whose existence they were up to now unaware, had, in fact, traversed the territories of both "clans" in their companies to link them into a single unit. One implication, of course, is that the Aranda people should not now be distinguishing their own from their mother's mother's "clan", as they would were the two "clans" in question totemically distinct. The mother's mother's "clan" is the mother-in-law "clan" in Aranda society. Under the new arrangement, however, the mother-in-law can be a woman in one's own "clan", and 'father's sister's daughter' can be wife. Under the old Aranda arrangement, by contrast, this woman was prohibited as a marriage partner.

Our converts now return home to their compatriots to spread the good news. Unfortunately for their purposes, these still-Aranda people are now faced with a contradiction: they are prohibited from marrying someone with a mother in their own "clan" and continue to look to someone in the father's mother's "clan" on their own generation. The now Kariera "clans", by contrast, are looking to exchange with the same "clan" in consecutive generations, that is, to marry someone with a mother in their own "clan". What this translates into is a stalemate, with both sides going off in opposite directions to find new marriage partners or with the Aranda sector eventually coming to accept the new totemic truths and themselves undergo conversion and transition. This actually poses no great problem since one form of society can become the other without any loss of adaptive advantage: the gains and losses of access to trading partners and resource areas by totemic company and marriage respectively still balance. Thus is the revolutionary inevitablity of the force of contradiction avoided. In a sense, the situation is little different from that in our own society where one Fall's fashion is readily exchanged for the next without risking nakedness.

Not only was an interest in the technological means of destruction virtually absent in Australia but also an interest in technological change as such. This was true even in the northern regions where the tools of 'progress' were also known from the Macassans. Graeme Pretty (1976), for instance, has observed that "Australian lithic traditions fail to exhibit the innovativeness and technical excellence of the European tradition." There is even a suggestion from the Tasmanian evidence that technological change was sometimes regressive! But rather than attribute this to the Australians' presumed primitiveness, as many of his fellow archaeologists have done, Pretty rather enquires "whether the disparity of quality between European and Australian lithic industries might not conceal a contrast between a society pre-occupied with technology and economy on the one hand and a soci-ety preoccupied with social experimentation and cosmogony on the other." Indeed!

* * * * *

In my kinline-confederation society I worry a great deal about instructing my "clanspeople" in the next generation, not only of how to make a living but also of their "clan" boundaries and the rules by which theirs is associated with other "clans". They must know where these jurisdictions lie and how they are inter-related. This blue-print cannot be allowed to vary in the minds of our young lest it begin to diverge from that in the minds of our neighbours. This means I must spend a great deal of time and trouble merely getting to and from ceremonies. I have to learn other dialects and languages so I can communicate with people there. I live in fear that someday I will arrive amongst people who will not understand what I have to say, or they will arrive to confront me. They may not respect my "clan's" claims and I will lose my lands, even my life. This makes it even more imperative that the young be properly indoctrinated. I will have to make them believe the ancestors return to every ceremony we perform to watch what we do and see that it is carried out correctly, and that transgressions are severely punished. So awful are the implications of a violation of the design for life, that, sadly for human life is precious, occasionally we must kill the frivolous and irresponsible for ignoring or making light of the rules. It is painful but it must be done, for future life depends on their death.

* * * * *

Nambirrirrma

The aboriginal myth of Nambirrirrma deals almost exclusively with the problem of communication. I have treated it elsewhere (1978a) but without its fundamental mythological structure in mind.

The myth is remarkable for its lack of opposition. Two men journey across Bickerton Island, meet a man who has descended from the sky, work out how they're related to him, bring back the people within whose territory they are situated, work out some more interrelations, provide him with a wife, then go home. The stranger has a son and later dies. Unless you know something of kinline-confederation principles, you wouldn't be aware that con-flict was even potential in this story, but it is.

Without going into great detail about the intricacies of inter"clan" relationships in the myth, let me just say that the story involves people in four "clans" -- A, B, C, and D. "Clan" A man sets out from his country (below) and moves along the beach toward "clan" B country. As he does, the stranger, Nambirrirrma, descends with the rain from the sky and sits down in B country. As A moves inland from the beach into B clan territory, he spots Nambirrirrma sitting there. He thinks perhaps he's a man from "clan" C.

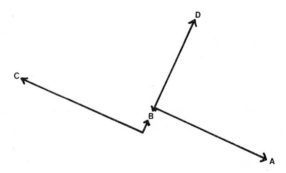

Figure 7.   Movements of Characters in the Nambirrirrma Tale in Relation to "Clan" Estates.

Meanwhile, a "clan" C man has, in fact, set out from his own country to go fishing in "clan" B territory.

The "clan" A man is certainly having a difficult time identifying the stranger. Perhaps he's from the mainland. He is certainly a different kind of person. Finally A asks him who he is and Nambirrirrma replies that he is "clan" B man. A then asks his name: "Nambirrirrma", he says. Then the "clan" A man spots "clan" C man approaching. He calls him over and asks him if he recognizes the stranger. He doesn't and suggests that Nambirrirrma might have come from God (the story is being told in 1969 after about a generation of mission contact). C asks Nambirrirrma what language he speaks and he replies, "our language".

Now it is Nambirrirrma's turn. He enquires of the whereabouts of the owners of "clan" B territory. A answers that they are over on the other side of the island with the people of their mother's "clan" (in this Aranda-like society this is the one they marry in alternate generations). C now shows Nambirrirrma the location of his own country, prompting Nambirrirrma to ask where "clan" B territory is, in fact, located. A shows him, then points out the location of his own territory. From all this Nambirrirrma concludes that A is his mother-in-law's clan. The "system" now begins to fall into place. A and B marry C and D in alternate generations (B marries C in Nambirrirrma's generation).

This settled, A tells Nambirrirrma he should be over in D territory with his own B people. But Nambirrirrma refuses to go. "Clan" A man offers to go and fetch them instead. Nambirrirrma agrees. "Clan" C man then goes home to fetch his own people.

When they return, B confirms Nambirrirrma's status and with A they arrange for him to take a wife from "clan" C. C meanwhile are camped separately by themselves on the beach. When they hear of these plans "clan" C protest, but to no avail. "Clan" A now tries to persuade Nambirrirrma to take either a woman with child, or two women. Nambirrirrma refuses. One young girl is what he wants and one young girl is what he gets. They marry, she has a child and Nambirrirrma dies.

What is potential in this tale but is never mentioned, let alone activated, is a claim to an estate on the basis of residence or occupation instead of totemic affiliation. "Clan" B's lands are vacant and "clan" A makes the first move to occupy them. He at least has some claim as a member of B's totemic fraternity (i.e., is in a "clan" B never marries). But then Nambirrirrma appears in the form of a mediator standing between A's and B's proper, standing between occupation and "clanship" as an ambivalent 'stranger/owner'. C's arrival is likewise mediated by Nambirrirrma who now successfully works out his relationship to these men and their "clans" in their terms. And yet he does not seem to know where his own "clan" estate lies.

Through the course of their conversation, A and C's ambitions are weakened by all admitting to the real nature of the "clan" alliance system as they attempt to work out Nambirrirrma's true identity. If Nambirrirrma is not who he claims to be then "clan" B land remains vacant but is now occupied by C and A. If he is who he claims to be then jurisdiction is established despite the presence of C and A. Now there is an attempt to remove the "clan" weakener and the mediator Nambirrirrma by persuading him to join his 'own' people on the other side of the island, itself a recognition of the "clan" principle. This possibility meets with opposition from Nambirrirrma which, in turn, resolves "clan" A man not to press the point further. He separates to "clan" D territory to fetch "clan" B people himself. C separates to fetch his own people.

Now representatives of all the "clans" return to B territory, but A, C, and D sit on the sidelines while Nambirrirrma and the B people establish their common identity. C are in the weakest position, being camped alone by themselves on the beach. A is weakened by being separated from the rest of his people, having opted instead to go and fetch the B and D people. C have the numbers to press a claim but would have to do so without the

A's and in opposition to B and their D allies. Of course it never comes to this: A collaborates with B, and C capitulates by allowing one of its women to go to Nambirrirrma. His job done, Nambirrirrma himself now separates, i.e., dies.

The proclivity of people in production group diversity/ kinline-confederation society for analytic thought is aptly demonstrated throughout the tale as each element in the society's blueprint is removed from its context, painstakingly examined, and then put back into place, all without anything being fundamentally altered. And how could it? In theory there is no problem to be 'resolved'.

I have suggested elsewhere that Nambirrirrma might in fact represent a Macassan visitor who actually performed a mediating function between aboriginal "clans" whose members were often away from their estates for long periods of time. The Macassans may have been unwitting mediators, however, with little idea of why they were associated with one "clan" or another. The Macassans simply came each year, and the Aborigines may merely have taken advantage of this situation -- even encouraged them to do so -- knowing full well that they would eventually sail back to their own country on the prevailing east wind at the end of each trading season.

The myth itself may have originated with the emigration of the Warnungwadarbalangwa from Bickerton to Groote Eylandt -- an actual historical event. They are, in fact, "clan" C, the "clan" that is singled out for special instruction. The departure of one "clan" on an island of four where it takes that many to make a system would represent an impending crisis of considerable magnitude.

Yandarranga

The story of Yandarranga, or Central Hill, is but one of the many myths I collected on Groote Eylandt in 1969 which had to be relegated to a trunk in my study as basically undecipherable. What I mean is that I could follow the story and, indeed, recounted it in my 1974 monograph, but, at that time, I did not understand it.

Like Nambirrirrma, Central Hill's is a travelling tale -- interminably boring and uneventful unless, of course, you are aware of the potential problem it is seeking, at all costs, not to mention. Research into what's not in a tale is, of course, an almost impossible task without as much knowledge of the context as the audience themselves.

Central Hill is, in myth, a mediator whose ability to link exclusive and otherwise unconnected jurisdictions is weakened by the exclusivity principle itself which ties him down to each "clan" he visits and which, once removed, allows opposition to (potentially) emerge between himself, and his fraternity-mates. But this eventuality is avoided by the participants -- including Central Hill -- separating and withdrawing one from the other.

Central Hill begins his journey on the mainland, travels to the coast, moves across to Bickerton Island, meets a blind woman, 'deposits' some children there, makes his way over to Groote Eylandt -- apparently against the wishes of this woman -- reaches the eastern part of the island and assumes his present form as the highest point on the horizon at 600' above sea level.

In so journeying, Central Hill connects up four local "clans" into an exogamous totemic company: the Ngalmi of the adjacent mainland, whose principal totem is Brown Snake; the Warnungamadada, Green Snake; the Wurrangilyanba, Parrott; and the Warnungangwurugwurigba, Central Hill itself.

Central Hill originated in the lands of the Nemamurdudi "clan" in central Arnhem Land. From there he moved eastward to Ngalmi territory where he sat down. But it was too dirty so he

went on to Warnungamadada country on the coast. But he kept
sinking down in the mud so he moved out into the sea and came
across to Warnungamadada country on Bickerton Island (where that
"clan" had been given an estate as an inducement to move over
from the mainland to take the place of the departing Warnungwadarbalangwa "clan" mentioned earlier). From there he cut across
land to Wurrangilyanba country where he 'threw out his anchor'
(i.e., landed, as in a canoe). While he was drying himself off
he again sank down in the mud, so he 'threw off some sons' to
make himself lighter so he could move on. At another place in
the same "clan's" territory he discarded some wild apples. There
he met the blind woman Dimimba and helped her dig up some yams
for food. But now he began to sink down into the mud again, so
much so that he could barely drag himself along.

So he left Dimimba and made his way across to Groote Eylandt
oblivious of the fact that Dimimba had gathered up her spears and
spear-thrower and was now hurling them at him from behind. She
missed; but where the spears struck the land, new places were
created. Then she began to gash her head until the blood flowed
(a sign of grief or of anger), so much so that it spilled into
the sea and washed all the way over to Groote Eylandt. Then she
returned to her own country with Central Hill's 'sons'. And the
'sons' spread the Anindilyaugwa language (the language of Bickerton Island and Groote Eylandt) everywhere. Then Dimimba covered
herself with a paperbark covering and finally sat down.

Meanwhile, Central Hill had reached a point on the coast of
Groote Eylandt belonging to the Warnungwudjaragba "clan" (situ-
ated in a different totemic company), though the actual spot
where he landed is said to belong to the Warnungangwurugwurigba.
Here he again began to sink down and so threw off some more
'sons'. These 'sons' told him to leave this place: "Go on to
Warnungangwurugwerigba country," they said. So he did, sitting
down there and making himself comfortable. Then he made Lake
Hubert (an inland sea) where he caught lots of fish. That's all:
"Ngawa bin'da."

Unless you know in advance that Central Hill is a totemic connector it is impossible to see the potential threats to him carrying out this function. A potential for settling down exists in each "clan" territory in turn, but each time it is overcome by Central Hill himself, though in the final analysis with some help from his sons. Here he seems in danger of confusing one place belonging to his "clan" with his "clan's" territory as such. The misapprehension is corrected and he moves on to his final resting place in the appropriate "clan" territory.

But it is with Dimimba that the dangers loom largest. Central Hill sinks down twice in her country and later enters into a co-production arrangement with her. This relationship is anomalous in all respects: cross-sex working relations occur only within marriage and these are two people _within_ the same totemic company. This relationship, in fact, contravenes _all_ the rules, the man helping the woman in her _gathering_ activities. Co-production as such is being raised as a basis for forming social relationships. So too Central Hill's sedentary tendencies. Central Hill's sedentary tendencies could also be interpreted as attempts to establish land rights by residence.

What, of course, is happening here is that the "clan" principle itself is being removed to allow him to complete his purpose and link these exclusive and otherwise isolated jurisdictions. But in so doing, all that this society is _not_, potentially looms on the horizon. But before that is realized -- before violence erupts within the fraternity -- the characters separate and withdraw. The spears that are thrown never reach Central Hill who continues on oblivious to the violent intentions. Dimimba misses because she's blind -- blind, perhaps, to Central Hill's true identity. There has to be an _excuse_, not a reason, for the potential coming into being.

For his part, by actually completing his journey, Central Hill implies some kind of unity amongst the "clans" he visits -- he deposits his 'sons' in various places and they go about instructing the 'world' in one language. The implication is avoided, however, in what would otherwise appear a paradoxical episode. It is Central Hill's <u>sons</u> who, in fact, insist that he move on and settle down in the estate of but one "clan", the "clan" that will henceforth name him their principal totem. Central Hill separates from his sons and withdraws, now being as remote and incommunicable as were the other "clans" before his journey. It is not without significance that it is Central Hill, not Dimimba, who is the tale's only non-human character, 'alien' with respect to the 'clans' he connects.

The mythological conclusion, 'separate and withdraw', is obviously one that can readily be translated into behaviour. And if we are to take the Australians' myths of the Macassans as intellectual attempts to come to terms with these visitors seriously, then 'separate and withdraw' is exactly what we would expect them to have done.

Midjanga

Originally, a Macassan ship and a European ship came up from the
south to Groote Eylandt, stopping at Golbamadja on the east coast
where the spirit of a Macassan is still said to live in a cave.
As they went on towards Bickerton Island they stopped at various
places - Dalimbo, Umbakumba, Djaragba and Badalumba -- and asked
the people there in the Macassan language, "What people are you?"
The natives, not understanding these words, merely repeated them
(an incident in the myth that evokes roars of laughter).   At
Bickerton Island, they repaired the Macassan ship and made it
very long so that it would sail quickly; the European ship needed
no repairs.   The Macassan ship proved to be too long, however,
and a portion was therefore cut off; this still remains at
Bickerton Island at Bandubanduwa.

The ship then went on to Melville Island (near Darwin,
called Lau or Lauwa by the Warnindilyaugwa).   There the people
know the Macassan language well, and the Macassans stopped and
made a huge fire that was blown by the north west wind all over
the mainland and over Groote, so that the people turned black.
Before that they were white or like half-castes.   The smoke
covered everything like a fog, and the Melville Islanders, being
right in the midst of the thickest smoke, became particularly
black.   Other tribes on the edges of the smoke-cloud were not so
strongly blackened.

*   *   *   *   *

This myth, recorded by Peter Worsley in 1953, opens with a
mediator -- the Macassan and European ships -- linking various
"clan" estates in the region, though in a very unconventional
fashion.   In reality, Dalimbo, Umbakumba, Djaragba and Badalumba
are in different totemic companies and exchange husbands and
wives.   But in the myth, ships link them all into one, theoretic-
ally unmarriageable, category.   The implication is symbolized
explicitly: before Blacks were Blacks everyone, including the
Europeans and Macassans, were white or like half-castes.   What's

more, the Macassans, if not the Europeans, are one with the
Aborigines in having a "clan" estate complete with all the spiritual attachments appropriate to its functioning.

The possibility of unity emerging is, then, the potential
problem dealt with by the myth. And, indeed, before 'unity'
emerges full-blown through incorporation of the Melville Islanders, it is replaced by diversity through separation: Smoke from
the Macassan's fire differentiates Blacks from Whites and Macassans, turning those Aborigines in closest contact with the inter-
lopers -- those speaking the Macassans' language at their point
of entry into Australia, the Melville Islanders -- more black
than the rest, i.e., more in need of separating from the cause of
the potential problem.

As in the Central Hill myth, indigenous "clan" weakeners
have been temporarily removed to expose a potential problem --
unification under the technologically superior Macassans and
Europeans -- only to be set back into place once their actual
presence has passed. Predictably, 'opposition' never emerges
full-blown even on a symbolic plane. Under the influence of
Macassans and Europeans, differences range from white to half
caste. After the ships have moved on they range from 'particularly black' to 'not so strongly blackened'. 'Black-white' may
be implicit, but it is never mentioned explicitly. What's more,
Macassans apparently retain their "clan" estate despite the
separation. This fits well with our knowledge of the actual
structure of Aboriginal-Macassan relations in this area.

The leading scholar on this aspect of Aboriginal history,
Campbell Macknight, maintains that through the contact period
(for 200 or so years to 1907 when the Australian authorities
finally banned their visits), "Macassans and Aborigines", the
"two cultures", seem to have existed "side by side involved
neither in major cooperation nor in competition." Lloyd Warner,
who worked in nearby north-east Arnhem Land, observed that the
Macassans themselves organized a policing system to prevent their
men from having contact with Aboriginal women. This coincides

nicely with the statement in the myth that it is the Macassans, not the Aborigines, who make the smoke which establishes a differentiation. On the other hand, on Groote Eylandt the Aborigines made a point of keeping their women secluded from contact and fitted them with bark dresses when association was unavoidable.

In sum, Aborigines and Macassans seem to have separated out one from the other in a relation of interdependence but with the Macassans occupying the superior position. They had the superior technology and would come whether the Aborigines liked it or not. The Aborigines assumed the position of a caste, then, rather than a "clan".

This 'ship-myth' was recorded just after intensive contacts with Europeans began. It recognizes the Europeans as the technologically superior people overall. Separation into interdependence also marked early Aboriginal-white relations, at least on the Aborigines' side. They refused to come into the mission established on Groote Eylandt in the late 1920s, preferring instead to deal through intermediaries for supplies and information. But, finally, when the mission moved itself inland in an effort to entice the Aborigines away from their traditional fishing preserves, they relented, setting themselves up in a grid pattern of camp sites separate from the missionaries' own semicircle of residences. And there they more or less have remained until today.

Down south, however, attempts at accommodation were far less successful. Where the Aborigines stood in the path of the settler and his ways they and their accomplishment were brutally trampled into the ground never to be heard from again.

*   *   *   *   *

Australian Aboriginal society can best be represented as two sets of intersecting parallel lines, the verticals expressing the "clan" totemic company dimension, the horizontals marriage alliance.

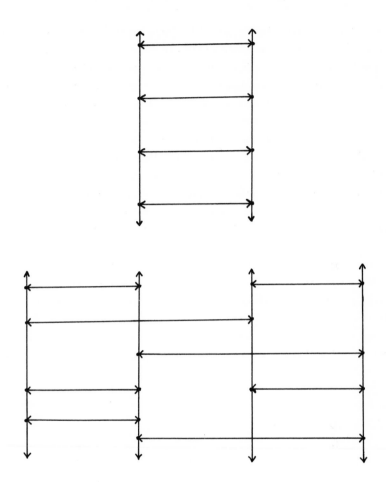

Figure 8. Abstract Representation of Base-two and Base-four
Aboriginal "Clan" Societies.

This is not only the form reached by a 'scientific' conclusion; it is also the way Aborigines express the essence of their
own way of life. Take their manner of depicting the sacred
design of "clanness". In the bark painting of Central Hill from
Groote Eylandt at the beginning of this Chapter we see verticals

interconnected by 'horizontal' herringbone and cross-hatched
lines representing sacredness itself.

Lest there still be doubt about the Aborigines' ability to
think as abstractly as the observer, consider this example: I
once asked an Aboriginal friend to diagramme his own 'kinship'
system. He set out five stones, three in a line one under the
other, another to the left of the one at the top, another to the
right of the one at the bottom. The line, he said, was his
"clan"; the stone at the top left was a woman in the "clan" his
own had married two generations ago; the stone on the bottom
right was a woman of the same "clan" which his generation should
also marry. This other 'line' was represented by the 'box' which
enclosed the display -- a comic book. His depiction is at least
the equal, if not the superior, of any anthropologist's to date.
Most of my colleagues depict his system as a symmetrical
sprawling-out of kinship ties from a single focal point called
'Ego'.

The lineal motif also dominates Aboriginal conceptions of
space as this drawing of Bickerton Island by one of my informants
illustrates:

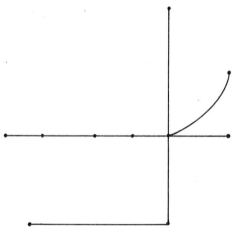

Figure 9. Galiawa's Drawing of Bickerton Island.

The straight lines represent the travels of mythological beings associated with the island's "clans" and the dots on the lines refer to their principal totemic sites.

Time in classic Aboriginal society is, objectively, cyclical, non cumulative, which is what you would expect in a society where the impetus for technological change and territorial expansion is absent. In Aboriginal theology, the spirit of a dead person doesn't so much <u>progress</u> from one domain to another of a better order, as <u>transfer</u> from one to another of the same type -- one that is a mirror image of itself. In some Aboriginal societies the spirit of the deceased is believed to return to his or her "clan" of origin to be born again into the world of humans, to die and be born again into the empirical world until adulthood is reached in which event it is allowed to proceed through to its final resting place in this parallel world of the ancestors and their totemic spirits.

PITJANTJATJARA

Locality-incorporative features are not entirely absent in the Warnindilyaugwa's way of life: their "clans" do allow co-residence as a means of acquiring "clan" membership but only under such exceptional circumstances as long-term prior association on the part of someone in the same company or the impending extinction of one's own "clan". It is not surprising that these features should be found here -- in theory it is what their way of life has overcome. The fact that the Groote Eylandters can imagine the implications of implementing these features as an alternative 'system', as in the Nambirrirrma myth, speaks for itself.

But it is amongst the Pitjantjatjara or Western Desert people where locality-incorporation is most pronounced. And yet, even here, the Western Desert way of life is so far beyond this arrangement as to leave even the Pacific West Coast Indians behind in its wake. Residence and incorporation do not in and of themselves determine relationships in the Western Desert either between people or between people and nature. The Idea of abstract, eternal jurisdiction always mediates, though here the jurisdictions in question are meandering lines of totemic sites, each affiliated with a particular totemic being, rather than the transluscent cubes of the Warnindilyaugwa. ✗

In the Western Desert, membership in the totemic juris-diction is determined not by the father or the mother but by place of birth. The child becomes a member of the jurisdiction within which he or she has quite literally fallen. However a child should be born within the father's jurisdiction and if s/he is not, suffers certain penalties: s/he can never be fully admitted into the inner life of the "clan" s/he adopts, though to compensate s/he is afforded free access to the "clan" of the father (i.e., the mother's husband), the man who should have fixed his or her totemic identity.

In the Western Desert, a man and a woman identify separately
as members of spouse-giving and spouse-taking jurisdictions
before marriage but 'merge' after marriage to refer to their
children by the same relationship terms: KADA (for males), undal
(for females). The couple -- and their respective "clans" --
seem to be incorporating on marriage as on the Pacific West
Coast. Furthermore, everyone on both the grandparents' and
grandchildren's generation are referred to by the same terms
irrespective of "clan". But this apparently band-enclosing-
"clan" feature, in contrast to the Canadian Indian situation,
rather derives from the fact that in the Western Desert all
totemic jurisdictions are linked into the same company by virtue
of the criss-crossing of all their respective Dreamtime tracks.
"Clans" do seem to incorporate on marriage but are singled out
again a few generations later when they again become eligible for
intermarriage.

Between the Pitjantjatjara and the Warnindilyaugwa -- quite
literally -- is an intermediate case, the Aranda, where
membership in the totemic "clan" is determined by place of conception and the father such that dual affiliation is allowed when
a person is conceived wrongly at a place outside the paternal
estate. Relationships, however, take their definition strictly
from "patriclan" membership as such.

It is where the kinline-confederational framework was consolidated least that we would expect warlike tendencies to be
most apparent. Tindale, in his Aboriginal Tribes in Australia
(the term 'tribe' really has no meaning in Australia except perhaps in the Western Desert), reports that ecological crises were
also social crises in the Western Desert, as amongst the Cree:

> To the west it was so dry that most of the Pitjant-
> jara tribespeople were forced to shift eastward and
> by 1916 had usurped the territory of the northern
> hordes of the Jankudjara, permanently driving them
> away from the eastern Musgraves. There was a
> forced southward shift of the Jankundjara people by
> from 140 to 160 miles (225 to 250 km) . . . Some of

the displaced hordes of the Jankundjara and a few
Antakirinja tribespeople moved southward and at-
tempted to live on the land of their former southern boundary and in the marginal strip between the
Kokata and Ngalea territory. Some years later,
when unable to move north again to the Everard
Range in a time of drought, they descended to Ooldea for the first time in the lives of the present
Jangkundjara. The Kokata who had long used Ooldea
as a western standby water refuge, which they
shared with other tribes, including the Wirangu,
thereupon moved eastward and settled near Tarcoola
where European settlements have since held them.

Again in theory this, the imperialist tendency, is the very
one that mature kinline-confederation transcends. But it is
worth noting that the Jangkundjara and Antakirinja, both organized in a fashion similar to the Pitjantjara, did find companion-
ship elsewhere.

*   *   *   *   *

In Western Desert mythology as in that of the Pacific West
Coast we once again encounter two logics of thought, although
here the one which 'proceeds' from mediation toward withdrawal
predominates over the other proceeding from opposition to the
illusion of a solution. This is precisely what we would expect
in a society where both kinline-confederation and locality-incorporation are highlighted but where the former predominates. We
might also expect what we also find here -- cannibal creatures!

Ma:mu

"They resemble," say Ronald and Catherine Berndt (1945), "human beings, but at times may assume various shapes, particularly that of the 'ngeni, a small bird. The male ma:mu is tall and heavily built with a massive head, his hair growing to a peak. His teeth are long, and bloody from biting and eating human beings; his nails are long; and he usually carries a large black club."

In one ma:mu story recorded by the Berndts in western South Australia, the giant ancestral being 'Tulina is out hunting and sees two 'ma:mu 'di:dji (females) which he tries to kill. He is able to catch one of them, but loses the other, not, however, before breaking its leg. He knows it cannot be far away. The one he captures he cooks and takes back to camp. As he approaches, his children rush out to see the ma:mu and break off one of its hands to eat. But their mother -- also a ma:mu -- sees what is happening and takes this 'meat' out of her children's grasp. The dead ma:mu is her 'sister's son'.

If we take cannibalism as a metaphor for the social process of incorporation here, as we did amongst the Cree, and interpret these spirits-in-human-form as relatively close 'others', then the episode makes immediate sense: 'Tulina is trying to incorporate two women by marriage who are in the wrong marriage category. As his wife's sister's children, they are on the generation adjacent to him in a "clan" closely related to his own. The rule in this Western Desert society is that you marry someone in your own generation but not in a "clan" yours has married over the last two generations.

As a mythological sequence, the opening scenario is bizarre indeed. We begin with a statement of opposition -- the killing of a member of another "clan". Then a potential opposition arises but it fails to materialize -- the actual incorporation of the too-close-other, first by 'Tulina and then by his children. Then follows separation -- of 'incorporator' from 'incorporatee'. In short, we begin with bits and pieces of two mythologics. The admixture continues.

'Tulina ignores his wife and continues feeding the cooked
ma:mu to his children. This realizes one potential extreme --
incorporation of the too-close-other -- though it is not as
extreme an act as it might have been had 'Tulina himself done the
incorporating. But then 'Tulina sets out alone to capture the
wounded ma:mu, apparently bent on realizing just this possibility. In fact, he seems to be moving toward an even more
extreme possibility. The myth is explicit: 'Tulina's breasts
immediately grow large and he suckles the children as would a
mother. On reaching the ma:mu cave he attempts to force his way
in to capture his prey. In other words, 'Tulina acts in disres-
pect of jurisdiction and attempts an incorporation which would
lead to self-reproduction.

But as he infringes upon their territory the ma:mu swarm out
to meet him. In mythological terms, opposition emerges now that
weakeners -- "clan" and conventional marriage rules -- have been
removed. The ma:mu pin him to the ground, pull out his penis and
testes and squeeze the milk from his breasts, as the ma:mu that
'Tulina has wounded demands. 'Tulina is thus unsexed to prevent
reproduction of any kind. At the same time 'Tulina's opposition
to the two ma:mu is also weakened. Not so the ma:mu, however.
They now set off to kill his children, appropriately substituted
for 'Tulina as potentially incorporating, self-reproducing
beings. Mediation follows. The 'mother's brothers' of the
children -- representing "clan" -- move to meet the ma:mu. But
the ma:mu have not been suitably weakened; the mediation is
doomed to fail. The mother's brothers are forced to fight the
ma:mu and kill many in the process. In protecting the children
the mother's brothers preserve their jurisdiction intact but
themselves become extreme in the process and preserve the children's original devious tendencies.

In the end some of 'Tulina's people are separated from some
of the ma:mu, predictably after opposition has been released by
the removal of weakeners, the last term in one mythological

scenario. But then there is the illusion of synthesis or resolution effected through the substitution of 'Tulina's children
for 'Tulina at one pole of the original opposition. That is the
final term in the other 'mythologic'. Actually, 'illusion of
synthesis' is perhaps a misnomer. The problem of 'Tulina's
<u>children's</u> original deviation is simply ignored.

Wadi Kutjara

The Wadi Kutjara are two ancestral men named Kurukadi and Mumba who are related as brothers-in-law. There is nothing anomalous about this. But the two possess a group of women known as Kunkarunkara. Some of these women are related to Mumba as 'sister's daughter's' and are thus ineligible to him as wives, being on the generation adjacent to his and seemingly in a "clan" his own has recently married. All, however, are eligible to Kurukadi.

The potential opposition that informs this tale, then, is Mumba's designs on these ineligible women. Immediately there appears on the scene a mediator, Kulu, who is in the same section as Kurukadi and therefore eligible to all the Wadi Kutjara's women. He is accompanied by a boy two generations his junior who is not only not eligible to the same women but is also too young to deviate even if he wanted to. It is their job to prevent the 'illegal' union of Mumba and the women -- to prevent incorporation based on what would be, in effect, co-residential association. In other words, it is their job to prevent locality-incorporation from becoming more pronounced than it already is.

This the Wadi Kutjara realize: they fear he will attempt to steal their women away. To prevent this possibility they tell the Kunkarunkara woman to "hide in the bush and prevent Kulu from seeing you". But now the Wadi Kutjara have weakened the integrity of their "band" and allowed Kulu to move into a mediating position, which he does.

When they finally meet, the Wadi Kutjara tell Kulu to "go that way to catch your meat", pointing in a direction opposite to the one the women have taken. But Kulu does not like being ordered about (taking orders is more appropriate to locality-incorporative society). Kulu goes his own way and eventually chances upon the women. But they refuse his advances and flee. He pursues them -- away from the Wadi-Kutjara. Thus mediated, the Wadi Kutjara and their women are prevented from uniting in space to form an incorporated whole.

Meanwhile the Wadi Kutjara journey eastward without their women. Then they turn to the north-east, then south and east to Kulardu and Kanba. Here they cut a slab of wood from the trunk of a mulga tree and fashion it into a tjurungga, an oval shaped sacred object. This they deposit in a cave nearby before moving on to describe a circle, beginning and ending at a place called Julardu. Both the tjurungga and this latter journey are arche-typal expressions of incorporative design; the lineal trips that precede this are more suggestive of kinline-confederation. The ambivalence evident here is explicit in the myth.

At Kurlardu the Wadi-Kutjara accidentally forget their spears, as is appropriate in a kinline-confederational society, but not their boomerangs, as befits locality-incorporative people: a superior form of technology is rejected but not weapons as such.

As all this is going on, Kulu is constantly on the Wadi Kutjara's minds. They suspect he has something to do with the women's disappearance. They turn north continuing on their journey and are about to give up all hope of ever seeing their women again when they spot Kulu just about to capture them. The women are tired from running and ready to capitulate. When they see the Wadi Kutjara they call out: "Our feet are sore; a man has chased us for such a long time." Not exactly a plea for rescue but it is enough for the Wadi Kutjara. They rush to their aid.

The geographical distance which has heretofore separated the Wadi Kudjara from the women is now removed and, predictably, con-sidering the nature of the 'mythologic' at issue, opposition emerges. The Wadi Kutjara attack Kulu with their boomerangs which fly toward him separating the ground into two hills as they do. Again, ambivalence is evident. Kulu is struck and dies from his wounds; and yet his mediation stands: "The woman did not continue with the Wadi Kutjara but journeyed independently to the north-east." The Wadi Kutjara move off in an opposite south-westerly direction: separation. But this is not the end of it.

At Talatala the Wadi Kutjara construct a <u>waningi</u>, a large ceremonial object made of string wound in circles around a cross of parallel sticks -- an intersection of incorporative and con-federative archetypes entirely appropriate in the circumstances.

Figure 10. Waningi at Taltala

At Taltala the two men perform a ceremony and circumscribe a lake -- evidence of locality-incorporative design? It would seem so considering what happens next in the tale:

The two men head north-east, in the <u>same</u> direction as their women. Along the way they see an eagle which they hunt and kill. But immediately Ngilamara appears on the scene and claims it as his own. The Wadi Kutjara insist it is theirs because they have killed it. Ngilamara becomes angry -- their claim is pos-sessory, his, apparently, proprietary -- and they fight. But the Wadi Kutjara are able to kill Ngilamara with their boomerang. Weakeners -- foreign jurisidiction -- removed, again opposition emerges. Locality-incorporation appears to be gaining the upper hand. The Wadi-Kutjara express the situation precisely: they throw their boomerang up into the air and it traces out a semi-

circle. Then they continue to the north-east, following the path
of their women.

But when they reach Winduru they move slightly eastward,
away from that path. The implications of the shift gain symbolic
expression: The Wadi Kutjara make two waningi, each somewhat
more lineal and less ovoid than their previous objects but with
two spirals emerging at either end, reminiscent of the Cree's
double-curvilinear motif.

Figure 11. Waningi at Kalkakutjara

These objects the Wadi Kutjara drag to Kalkakutjara, the
'two shoulders' place, which, in its duality, appears a sign of
the impending victory of kinline-confederation.

In the final episode of the tale the Wadi Kutjara approach a
group of men performing an initiation ceremony. One of the Wadi
Kutjara throws his boomerang up into the air and it traces out an
arc, returning to the other Wadi Kutjara. At this obvious sign
of locality-incorporative intent the performers flee --
separate. The Wadi Kutjara move on and finally climb into the
sky in the far east to become stars forever separated but in

complementary relation to their women who have in the meantime become the Pleiades.

In this myth, then, the first term in one mythological sequence, opposition, comes into being only to be overtaken by another ending in separation -- the logic appropriate to kinline-confederation.

* * * * *

In sum, what we have located here, amongst the Canadian Indian and the Australian Aborigines, are two distinct, though not opposed, ways of life, ways of thinking, ways of symbolizing, which find their clearest expression amongst two particular peoples widely separated in space if not in time -- the Cree and the Warnindilyaugwa. But even here some overlap exists: the Cree think somewhat along Warnindilyaugwa lines in some circumstances and go some way to grasping their Idea of heritable jurisdiction; the Warnindilyaugwa allow some measure of incorporation by co-residence and imagine a full-blown Cree world as an alternative to their own. And on each continent the contrasting features at issue become less pronounced the more we investigate the full range of variation there.

As the Pacific West Coast evidence suggests, we have an Algonkian people on the verge of becoming Australian; and the Pitjantjatjara evidence suggests an Australian people just having 'unbecome' (not yet become?) Algonkian. What is puzzling in this connection is why there are no Australians _per se_, on the Pacific West Coast, no Algonkians _per se_ in Australia.

We can perhaps understand why there are no Australians on the Pacific West Coast of Canada. The "clan"-federative tendency could not emerge full-blown so long as locality-incorporative features continued to operate in a systematic fashion, and they would continue to operate in a systematic fashion until the "clan"-federative tendency emerged full-blown. And even if it did emerge, it is abstract, fragmented, peaceful, withdrawing and vulnerable to attack -- by the very forces which brought it into being. On the Pacific West Coast the 'Australians' simply could not escape their neighbours -- or themselves.

How is it then that the Warnindilyaugwa, and with some qualification a whole continent of people, were not overtaken by the 'enemy', i.e. by similar tendencies within themselves? One could argue that they have been -- by Europeans. But still the outline survives in parts of the continent.

Perhaps kinline-confederation originated in South-East Asia and was carried to Australia across the land bridge that formerly linked the two continents many thousands of years ago. The Australians would then have been protected from their pursuers by the waters that flooded in to swamp their means of entry -- proverbial Israelites fleeing the Egyptians across the parted waters of the Red Sea. On the other hand, perhaps the accomplishment occurred within Australia, the harsh environment as such replacing locality-incorporation as the threat that forced people permanently into institutionalized interdependence. On the Pacific West Coast, at least, no such threat existed.

Then again, perhaps a new plane of existence was achieved through plain choice, the actors being aware of the forces moving them toward destruction and taking practical steps to prevent it.

In the first Book of Genesis we discern the outlines of a particular scenario -- a society unbecoming Australian and moving into another stream of existence whose predominant features are 'locality-incorporative'. However, it moves while retaining at least one Idea from its past. And that only compounds the society's problems.

A THEORETICAL INTERLUDE

THE LAWS OF HISTORY

The laws by which the Algonkians -- people in locality-incorporative society -- move and think and which bring the Australians
-- kinline-confederation -- into being, can be formalized and
summarized. Indeed, I gave some of them formal definition in my
discussion of locality-incorporation when I invoked the Marxist
scenario of a contradiction between the forces and relations of
production as appropriate to an understanding of change within
these parameters. I also pointed out that thought proceeds from
opposition in societies where opposition -- either on a horizontal or vertical plane -- is real and fundamental to the nature of
the society.

With reference to the emergence of another possibility out
of this scenario I spoke of threats that forced people into interdependence and of thought that proceeded from a mediated
universe where opposition had been tamed to end in separation and
withdrawal once it discovered the potentials lurking within its
midst. The Shamattawa Cree, in their Windigo myth, spoke of the
possibility that certain aspects of their society were, perhaps,
a negative response to a threat from outside. In the end they
decided that they weren't, but the question they posed at least
proceeded from the correct term if an alternative to their own
society is what they really had been after. 'Threat' is the
colloquial term; the proper technical term is anti-thesis. Its
place in the theoretical scheme of things is this:

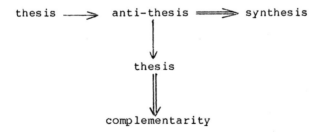

In its proper place, <u>anti-thesis</u> or negation is the theoretical reason why the Warnindilyaugwa and others like them should not exist.

Monism

The scenario running horizontally across the page (above) will, of course, be immediately familiar to my academic readers as the Hegelian/Marxist dialectic. Stated in general terms, 'something's existence is first asserted, then threatened by another's existence, overcomes it, is overcome by it, or the two merge together into a larger whole'. This process we can call monism, for the many are continually reduced to one by incorporation. Within the framework of human existence one might put it as follows: 'me $\longrightarrow$ you $\Longrightarrow$ me over you, you over me, us'. In this scenario the Idea of my/our jurisdiction or mine/ours over yours emerges. This is the political dimension stressed by the philosopher Hegel.

The economic dimension located by Marx follows along these lines:

technical means $\longrightarrow$ social relations $\Longrightarrow$ new mode of production
of production   of production   combining new social
                                                              relations with real-
                                                              ized technological
                                                              potential

Translated it reads: 'technology is always capable of benefitting more people than the existing relations of production will allow. Classes vie with one another within society for control of these benefits. The advantaged class overcomes the disadvantaged, the disadvantaged overcomes the advantaged, or the two merge together into a new whole'.

The human, political and economic dimensions together create the impression of an ego-centred, singular universe in which autonomy and self-sufficiency are driving forces -- as in locality-incorporative society. And, indeed, this is why, perhaps, technology appears first in the economic order of things -- the means to these ends on an individual or collective basis. The anthropologist Claude Lévi-Strauss has located a mode of thought which seems to me intrinsic to, or at least predominant within, such an order. Its logic runs,

opposition ⟶ weakening ⟶ mediation ⟹ illusion of
systhesis or
solution

Translated: 'in an attempt to resolve oppositions that are real (thesis ⟶ anti-thesis) thought seeks to avoid the revolutionary implications by substituting weaker terms for each pole in the opposition through a process of analogical reasoning which allows for the appearance of a mediator to effect the illusion of a resolution of the original opposition.'

This mode of thought Lévi-Strauss sees reflected in myth, though others have also seen it reflected in Western literature.

Pluralism

The scenario running vertically down the page in the first formu-
lation will be less familiar; indeed, I would think that it is
totally unfamiliar if not bewildering. <u>Anti-thesis</u> is negation,
nothing. How can something proceed from nothing? At this point
let us merely take it as something proceeding from the <u>threat</u> of
becoming nothing. Then, perhaps, we can translate the scenario
into human, political, economic and cognitive terms. '<u>Anti-
thesis</u> ─> <u>thesis</u> ══> <u>complementarity</u>', then, translates as:
'Under threat of annihilation by another, potential victims, each
to maintain themselves intact, are moved toward accommodation,
even toward accommodation with the threat itself. Under these
conditions the Idea of mutually respected jurisdictions feder-
atively interrelated emerges.'

This process we can call pluralism which is simply the many
maintained as many, in short, confederation. This is not to be
confused with mere fragmentation where the many are present but
are structurally unrelated. The human dimension to pluralism is
this, '<u>you</u> ─> <u>me</u> ══> <u>you and me</u>'. Here, the 'other' is
posed first, before self.

The economic dimension, as a spin-off from the monist
scenario, is this:

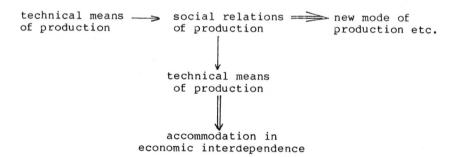

technical means ─> social relations ══> new mode of
of production   of production   production etc.

                           │
                           ▼
                    technical means
                    of production
                           ‖
                           ⇓
                    accommodation in
                economic interdependence

Translated: 'under threat, or with mutually respected jurisdictions in place, consideration of people's respective positions in
the production process takes precedence over technological change

as such. People are separated into interdependence, each to his
or her or their own (people, resources, functions). Human accommodation now becomes the driving force in history with technology
assuming a secondary role in the process.'

The logic of thought that accompanies this scenario is,
again, a spin-off from the monist scenario:

opposition $\longrightarrow$ weakening $\longrightarrow$ mediation $\Longrightarrow$ illusion of synthesis

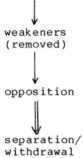

weakeners
(removed)

opposition

separation/
withdrawal

This can be translated as: 'in response to opposition that may
potentially emerge to undermine complementarity, thought inserts
mediators to stand on guard while the elements of the arrangement
are dissected and analysed in an effort to reach the root of the
potential problem. But in so doing, the weakeners that maintain
the arrangement intact must be removed and, once they are,
opposition that was heretofore merely potential all of a sudden
appears real. Thought separates and withdraws from its terms.'

The human, political and economic dimensions here create the
impression of an alter-oriented, plural universe in which accommodation and interdependence are stabilizing forces -- as in
kinline-confederation society. In theory, this scenario flows
negatively from a threat to (mutual) existence or positively from
mutually respected jurisdictions once formally constituted and
held together by mediators.

DERIVATION OF THEORY

The identity of the second scenario and its relation to the first emerged from an experiment with the terms of the Hegelian/Marxist dialectic in interplay with my research on Australian/Cree and elsewhere, notably Confederated Canada. My work on the Australians, following Lévi-Strauss, had shown, as we have already seen, how apparently different societies could be merely recombinations of the same basic elements and relations. And if societies why not theories. I began playing with the terms of the Hegelian/Marxist dialectic: 'anti-thesis $\longrightarrow$ thesis $\Longrightarrow$ synthesis', but this netted nothing in reality that I could fathom. 'Synthesis $\longrightarrow$ thesis $\Longrightarrow$ anti-thesis' was equally fruitless. But 'synthesis $\longrightarrow$ anti-thesis $\Longrightarrow$ thesis' was a different matter. This seemed to imply a unity 'deconstructing' into its component parts, though precisely how wasn't clear.

However, when I substituted human terms for each of the terms in these abstract formulations and reversed the first two terms of the Hegelian/Marxist dialectic (I $\longrightarrow$ you) I derived a completely new conclusion: 'you $\longrightarrow$ me $\Longrightarrow$ you and me'. To entertain that thought was to undergo a loss of self in identity with the other -- to experience anti-thesis first-hand -- and in this to experience a reaffirmation of self back through the other, ending as an indivisible, un-unifiable two.

The implication of this manipulation of the generative sequence of terms in the Hegelian/Marxist dialectic was obvious; if reversals in one instance generated a completely new conclusion reversals in others might do likewise. The 'other'conclusions I more or less knew: the people I was puzzling over at the time were certainly accommodating rather than competitive or even co-operative, and many of their texts ended 'unsatisfactorily' with the characters separating and withdrawing from each other and from issues. This new insight might tell me the steps that led up to these endings. And, in fact, I found it to work -- the data fit the generative sequences I had deduced. It was as simple as that. Now not only my Australian/Cree comparison but also my Australian material as such made more sense than it had before. I was able to resurrect all that undecipherable material I had relegated to my trunk. Even the conclusions now clarified themselves. And, yet not everything was clear.

I could imagine variations on a theme -- common enough in music; even a theme from variations -- my colleague Godfrey Ridout's composition, George the Third, his lament (culminating in "The British Grenadiers" minus its final note!). But themes from a variation? -- ending in 'complementarity' in one stream, 'synthesis' in another. And could the stream ending in 'complementarity' possibly trace the course of that most improbable of all logics, a non-binary dialectic, an anti-dialectic that promises to arrest the 'normal' course of historical events? Then there was the vexing question of how something could proceed from nothing. Threat fulfilled seemed to offer little hope for complementarity in any form. And yet there were the Australians.

*   *   *   *   *

In describing the terms of this theory I have been very careful in my choice of words. But it is inevitable that ambiguities should remain. This is partly due to the nature of the reality at issue. But it is also because conventional English is inadequate to convey my meaning, particularly the meaning of the terms of the dialect of pluralism. In this domain, English usages are particularly impoverished.

The exceptions, curiously are the terms monism and pluralism themselves. The Oxford English dictionary defines 'pluralism' as "a system that recognizes more than one ultimate principle", and 'monism' as "a system that recognizes but one." Movement toward two, movement toward one -- the essense of the difference between the two dialectics -- is thus readily communicated.

But when we come to the key concept 'complementarity', the dictionary is of very little use to us for 'complementary' is given as "serving to complete", and 'complement' as "that which completes". But what I mean by 'complementarity' is SOMETHING OF THE ONE EMBEDDED IN THE OTHER AND VICE VERSA WITHOUT LOSS OF INTEGRITY OF EITHER. This is also a good starting point for a definition of interdependent. But in the dictionary, 'interdependent' simply means "dependent on each other". 'Federate' (or confederate -- I will use the two synonymously here), which to my mind builds on the previous two, in the dictionary means, "band together in league for some common object." This is precisely the opposite of what I wish to communicate by the word. It implies incorporation as a process, a process endemic to the monist scenario, that is, 'synthesis'. By 'federate', then, I mean, INSTITUTIONALIZED COMPLEMENTARITY THROUGH THE IDEA OF ABSTRACT JURISDICTION IN THE PLURAL. 'Accommodation' fares better in its dictionary meaning: "settlement, compromise, adaptation". But under 'accommodate' we also read: "harmonize, reconcile", that is, meanings more appropriate to monism.

Such a confounding under the same word of what to me are incompatible meanings is perhaps confirmation of the thesis that there are two sides to existence, but it also bespeaks a civilization in which the two have not been adequately delineated, let alone evaluated. The reason is not hard to fathom: we have so far been dominated by the reality of only one of the scenarios in question.

The consequence is that I have to invent my own meanings for some of the terms and risk not so much being misunderstood as being ignored. Ignored because it will be hard work for the reader 'trained' in conventional ways of thinking and concepts to understand what I mean. Hence one of the reasons for integrating my analyses within a retelling of the texts. Somehow a story is easier to digest.

Concepts in the monist stream -- opposition, contradiction, synthesis, unity -- however, can all be understood in their conventional meanings, although it is perhaps worth specifying that in my usage, opposition only becomes contradiction when the two mutually exclusive elements in question are actually engaged in thought or reality.

Where understanding is likely to be most difficult is when I compound terms from both streams in order to communicate my meaning. The two I have in mind are 'complementary opposition' and 'opposed complementarity'. 'Complementary opposition' implies that elements once opposed are now in the process of being rendered complementary -- as in the Cree and Pacific West Coast Indians trying to become 'Australian'. Opposed complementarity is complementarity achieved but where opposition of a kind is re-emerging -- as in the Australian example above where Kariera and Aranda are 'opposed' but in such a way that one system can be substituted for the other without experiencing revolutionary upheaval. The apparently trivial difference between these two concepts -- merely a transposition of words -- may very well be the most important difference in the world.

Another reason why the concepts I will use are difficult to define in English is that 'English' insists on formal, static definitions for what are in reality processes.

GENESIS

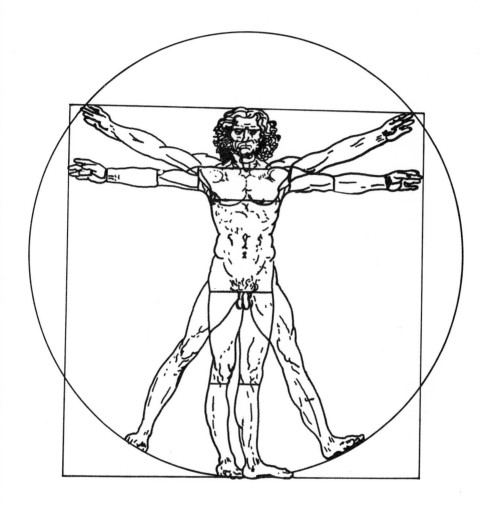

Figure 12.   Anatomical Proportions, Leonardo Da Vinci

GENESIS, THE READING

The reading that follows consists not only of episodes from the text of Genesis in its King James Bible translation but also the understanding which flowed from the initial reading through the theory in question. This I inserted back into the body of the text as unnumbered passages in a style commensurate with the style of that text to, in a sense, fill in the 'gaps' in the original.

If meaning is all that interests you, then simply read the central column, the body of the text, against the original or any other interpretation. If you are also interested in the interpretive process, then read the page three-dimensionally, simultaneously down the middle and each side of the page. On the weak, female, left side you can, from time to time, follow the pluralist aspect of the text in all its intricacies and dimensions; on the strong, male, right side you can follow the monist aspect of the text, again a complex unfolding. Indeed most of the texts dealt with thus far could have been organized in a similar fashion.

There are two sides to everything but Genesis, it appears, would there were only one -- the left-hand side:

(1)

According to ancient Hebrew tradition, 'in the beginning God created the heaven and the earth.' Small "h" small "e" heaven and earth -- a potential coming into being. What form would the becoming take? Would the two be separate and interdependent?, separate and antagonistic?, or one?

Within Creation moved two primary forces, the other finally coming to predominate over the one:

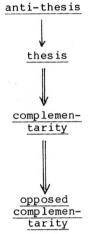

anti-thesis 2 And the earth was without form and void; and darkness was on the face of the deep. And the spirit of God moved upon the face of the waters.

thesis 6 And God said, Let there be a firmament in the midst of the waters, and let it divide the waters

complemen-tarity 7 And God made the firmament, and divided the waters which were under the firmament from the waters which were above and the firmament: and it was so.

8 And God called the firmament Heaven. And the evening and the morning were the second day.

opposed complemen-tarity 9 And God said, let the waters under heaven be gathered together unto one place, and let the dry land appear: and it was so.

10 And God called the dry land Earth; and the gathering together of the waters called he Seas: and God saw that it was good.

The threat of nothingness has hastened the becomings into being and is forming them into a complementarity, a plurality. At the same time, new elements of Creation are bringing forth their opposites:

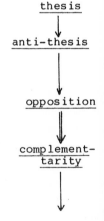

2   darkness   thesis

3 And God said, Let there be light: and there was light.   anti-thesis

4 And God saw the light, that it was good: and God divided the light from the darkness.

5 And God called the light Day, and the darkness he called Night. And the evening and the morning were the first day.   opposition

    Opposition is overcome as a force in Creation   complement-tarity

and the Earth and the Seas are now ready to receive

life.

11 And God said, Let the earth bring forth grass,
the herb yielding seed, and the fruit yielding
fruit after his kind, whose seed is in itself, upon
the earth: and it was so.

12 And the earth brought forth grass, and herb
yielding fruit, whose seed is in itself, upon the
earth: and it was so.

13 And the evening and the morning were the third
day.

Then God makes doubly sure that opposition is

subdued by placing a part of the one in the other:

14 And God said, Let there be lights in the
firmament of the heaven to divide the day from the
night; and let them be for signs, and for seasons,
and for days, and for years.

complemen-
tarity

15 And let them be for lights in the firmament of
the heaven to give light upon the earth: and it
was so.

16 And God made two great lights; the greater
light to rule the day, and the lesser light to rule
the night: and he made stars also.

complementary
opposition

17 And God set them in the firmament of the heaven
to give light upon the earth.

18 And to rule over the day and over the night,
and to divide the light from the darkness: and God
saw that it was good.

A sameness is first confounded by difference then a difference is confounded by sameness: opposed complementarity/com-
plementary opposition -- the fruit whose seed is within itself.

19 And the evening and the morning were the fourth day.

The Earth and the Seas are now ready to receive intelligent
life. There issue forth creatures of the Sea and of the Sky, and
the great whales.

23   And the evening and the morning were the fifth day.

Then   comes   life   in   God's   image,   abstract   intelligence
embodied   in   the   form   of   two   persons: male   and   female   T(he)y
create them.

> 28   Be fruitful and multiply, and replenish the
> earth and subdue it: and have dominion over the
> fish of the sea, and over the fowl of the air, and
> over every living thing that moveth upon the earth.

But theirs is to be a peaceable dominion: not animalkind
but the herb bearing seed and the seed bearing fruit are given as
'meat' for food.   Of this would animalkind also eat.   Intelligent
life would live in respect of Creation.

31   And the evening and the morning were the sixth day.

(2)

On   the   seventh   day   God   rests   and   reflects;   and   T(he)y
discover   a   flaw   in   Creation: In   the   beginning   was   the   waters
which subdivided into complementarity to overcome the opposition
potential between the two -- darkness and light.   In the beginning was One.   One is the fulfilment of opposition = synthesis =
merger.   Monism,

thesis ——> anti-thesis ====>

But revolution is in contempt of Creation.   And the Creation
of humankind is also recalled:

> 5 And every plant of the field before it was in
> the earth, and every herb of the field before it
> grew: for the LORD God had not caused it to rain
> upon the earth, and there was not a man to till the
> ground.
>
> 6 But there went up a mist from the earth, and
> watered the whole face of the ground.
>
> 7 And the LORD God formed man of the dust of the
> ground, and breathed into his nostrils the breath
> of life; and man became a living soul.

No flaw here: man's origins lie in the firmament, in the
waters already divided to rise as mist and fall as rain to still
the dust and breathe back life after the dust was raised into the
atmosphere. Man's origins are in two, not one.

But what of the place wherein man dwells?

> 8 And the LORD God planted a garden eastward in
> Eden; and there he put the man whom he had formed.
>
> 9 And out of the ground made the LORD to grow
> every tree that is pleasant to the sight, and good
> for food; the tree of life also in the midst of the
> garden, and the tree of knowledge of good and evil.
>
> 10 And a river went out of Eden to water the gar-
> den; and from thence it was parted, and became into
> four heads.

And one stream watered the garden of Havilah, where there is
gold, bdelium and onyx; and another flowed to Ethiopia, a third
to Assyria, the fourth to Euphrates.

Eden is not alone. Within Eden a resource is forbidden --
that it may be consumed elsewhere? Minerals for fruit? Five
interdependencies? What is certain, is that self-sufficiency
within the garden is forbidden. Oneness with the garden is
forbidden -- there is no error here.

But man is alone in the garden.

> 18   And the LORD God said, It is is not good that
> the man should be alone; I will make him an help
> meet for him.
>
> 21   And the LORD God caused a deep sleep to fall
> upon Adam, and he slept: and he took one of his
> ribs, and closed up the flesh instead thereof:
>
> 22   And of the rib, which the LORD God had taken
> from man, made he a woman, and brought her unto the
> man.

Woman whose source lies within man -- does she represent
oneness?   Is there an error here?   But woman is born of a part
withdrawn from man, that which he now lacks to make him whole.
Woman is a force against oneness, as much as she is a force for
oneness:

> 24   Therefore shall a man leave his father and his
> mother, and shall cleave unto his wife: and they
> shall be one flesh.

No, the error is that man and woman came from within the
same garden.   The error is that two persons, in the plural, and
the garden are one, have shared the same element.   And the error
is real.   Intelligent life must know it and grasp the implications.   That lot falls to woman;   Adam has the good fortune to be
asleep during the experience.

(3)

> 6   And when the woman saw that the tree was good
> for food, and that it was pleasant to the eyes, and
> a tree to be desired to make one wise, she took of
> the fruit thereof, and did eat.

If the garden can be self-sufficient in one way it can be
self-sufficient in others.   Eve shares her knowledge with Adam.

He also eats. Now they both know. Eve has returned Adam's gift; they are now complementary but opposed as male to female:

> 7   And the eyes of both of them were opened, and
> they knew that they were naked:

The _thesis_ that self-sufficiency is possible is contradicted by the _anti-thesis_ of the forbidden fruit, then _resolved_ into oneness by partaking of it. The error is compounded.

Man and woman now know half the Truth about Creation -- about the destructive force subordinated within it. Would they come to know more? Only if they are to experience it. But _pluralism_ is now a subordinate force, a subordinate _reality_ within the garden. It can be grasped only vaguely, even by God-like intelligence. When Adam and Even move out of the garden, they are moved by the force of imperfectly thought pluralism, the 'mythologic' of pluralism. It is this alone they experience and know, not pluralism itself:

mediation
(a bringing
together
without in-
terdepen-
dence)

> 1   Now the serpent was more subtil than any beast of the field which the LORD God had made. And he said unto the woman, Yea, hath God said, Ye shall not eat of the fruit of the tree of the garden?
>
> 2   And the woman said unto the serpent, We may eat of the fruit of the trees of the garden:
>
> 3   But of the fruit of the tree which is in the midst of the garden, God hath said, Ye shall not eat it, neither shall ye touch it, lest ye die.
>
> 4   And the serpent said unto the woman, Ye shall not surely die:

weakener
(a common-
ality that
really
isn't in
common)

> 5   For God doth know that in the day ye eat thereof, then your eyes shall be opened, and ye shall be as gods, knowing good and evil.

To weaken Eve's resolve the serpent, mediating God and humankind, Eve and Adam, asserts a false

commonality between them all: if humans and God are
likewise intelligent, then why should humans not
know that which God knows? But the identity is
false: humans, like God, have the intelligence to
know what they experience, but only God has experienced Creation, therefore humans can never know what
God knows. With the attempt to be as God, humans
merely come to perceive the destructive side of
Creation - monism. Opposition now begins to re-
emerge within Creation, between God and Creation,
between the different life forms of Creation:

'opposition' 14 And the LORD said unto the serpent, Because thou
(complemen- hast done this, thou art cursed above all cattle,
tarity and above every beast of the field; upon thy belly
drifting shalt thou go, and dust shalt thou eat all the days
apart) of thy life:

15 And I will put enmity between thee and the
woman, and between their seed and her seed; it shall
bruise their head, and thy shalt bruise his heel.

By the same token, woman will suffer as the
sexual object of man and be forced to endure the
pains of childbirth:

16 Unto the woman he said, I will greatly multiply
thy sorrow and thy conception, in sorrow thou shalt
'opposition' bring forth children; and thy desire shall be to thy
husband, and he shall rule over thee.

For his part, man must suffer the pain of toil
necessary to maintain life:

17 cursed is the ground for thy sake, in sorrow
'opposition' shalt thou eat of it all the days of thy life.

18 Thorns also and thistles shall it bring forth to
thee; and thou shalt eat the herb of the field;

19 In the sweat of thy face shalt thou eat bread,
till thou return unto the ground; for out of it wast
thou taken: for dust thou art, and unto dust shalt
thou return.

Under sway of the force of monism the children
of Creation -- man and woman, humankind and intelligent nature -- are at best opposed first, complementary second, at worst mutually destructive --
primarily the objects of each other's desires. The
future of Creation is no longer at best complementary before opposed.

But it is God, not humankind, who unleashes the
forces of destruction implicit in the new situation. The flaw, after all, lies in the Act of
Creation itself.

21   Unto Adam also and to his wife did the LORD God
make coats of skins, and clothed them.

Animals have been killed to cover up humankind's nakedness, at once at act of violence un-
leashing monism and a sign of something else, something now hidden under the surface beneath monism
still waiting to be 'known'.

But despite humankind's claim to God-like intelligence, that Truth will never be known:

22   And the LORD God said, Behold, the man is become
as one of us to know good and evil: and now, lest
he put forth his hand, and take also of the tree of
life, and eat, and live forever:

23   Therefore the LORD God sent him forth from the
Garden of Eden, to till the ground from whence he
was taken.

And so humankind withdraws from the garden
thinking they have all its secrets:

withdrawal-
separation

24   So he drove out the man; and he placed at the
east of the garden of Eden Cherubims, and a flaming
sword which turned every way, to keep the way of the
tree of life.

The force which had expelled them was this: 'mediation—>
weakener —> "opposition" ==>withdrawal-separation', or imperfectly thought pluralism. For withdrawal-separation is merely
the illusion of pluralism -- two existent but without relationship or connection. Of this humankind now has experience and
therefore knowledge. But the Secret of Life remains hidden.
Monism, now the predominant practice to be experienced, is death
and destruction.

Outside the garden, 'oneness', unity, prevails,

> 1 And Adam knew Eve his wife; and she conceived,
> and bare Cain and said, I have gotten a man from
> the LORD.

And indeed she has -- the embodiment of T(he)ir mistake.

A tradition of territorial self-sufficiency now comes into
being; a host of related sub-forces are set in motion which will
propel man and woman and their descendents, in whatever garden
they choose to occupy, on a tortuous journey through the present
in search of a future only dimly represented as The Word. The
principal of these forces is the drive for technological development -- the means of extracting more and more from the limited
resources at one's disposal, to feed a growing population without
expanding one's territorial holdings and so to remain self-
sufficient as a people.

The real error in Creation, then, is the isolation of Eden
from the four, whether fruit hoarded from minerals or minerals
from water, we shall never know. And once isolated and bound to
self-sufficiency, Eden suffered crises in resources and population and her people were moved.

(4)

Life outside Eden at first translates into an internal
struggle between the technical means of production and the social

relations of production -- between technological progress and individual inheritance. Life at first translates into the problem of Cain and Abel:

> 2 And she again bare his brother Abel. And Abel was a keeper of sheep, but Cain was a tiller of the ground.

Cain is firstborn and successor to Adam; but he comes by the older technology, cultivation. Abel, the second born, comes by the more recent technology, herding, but does not succeed. Progress dictates that the more recent technology succeed in the interests of achieving self-sufficiency. But with Cain's succession, cultivation will predominate. Progress dictates that the social relations of production must be overthrown, but Cain kills Abel to remain Adam's successor and prevents it.

But now the superior mode of production embodied in Abel is also destroyed. This is no solution. Cain is banished and doomed to wander in foreign lands. He marries into the land of Nod where he remains a poor cultivator forever inferior to the local inhabitants. And yet in this state he breeds a new set of possibilities: Jabal, father of nomads and herders; Jubal, father of musicians; and Tubalcain, father of craftsmen in brass and iron. But of what avail are these interdependencies to Adam and Eve who are now alone in their own lands and facing the problem of self-sufficiency? They must try again.

> 25 And Adam knew his wife again; and she bore a son, and called his name Seth: For God, said she, hath appointed me another seed instead of Abel, whom Cain slew.

Seth is 'first born' representing Abel. One successor is the solution to Cain and Abel, but 'one' alone cannot be risked as a future and indeed is the source of the problem.

(5)

And Seth begat sons and daughters, and his seed begat sons and daughters. And the problems of the world were great.

(6)

4 There were giants in the earth in those days; and also after that, when the sons of God came into the daughters of men, and they bare children to them, the same became mighty men which were of old, men of renown.

5 And GOD saw that the wickedness of man was great in the earth, and that every imagination of the thoughts of his heart was only evil continually. **opposition** (among men and between God and man)

6 And it repented the LORD that he had made man on the earth, and it grieved him at his heart.

7 And the LORD said, I will destroy man whom I have created from the face of the earth; both man, and beast, and the creeping thing, and the fowls of the air; for it repenteth me that I have made them.

8 But Noah found grace in the eyes of the LORD.

mediation

9 Noah was a just man and perfect in his generations.

14 Make thee an ark of gopher wood: rooms shalt thou make in the ark, and shalt pitch it within and without with pitch.

17 And, behold, I, even I, do bring a flood of waters upon the earth, to destroy all flesh, wherein is the breath of life, from under heaven; and every thing that is in the earth shall die.

18 But with thee will I establish my covenant; and thou shalt come into the ark, thou, and thy sons, and thy wife, and thy sons wives with thee. **solution?**

But Noah's wife and his sons' wives are the daughters of men!; they are the source of wickedness. But without them Noah's line cannot reproduce.

19 And of every living thing of all flesh, two of
every sort shalt thou bring into the ark, to keep
them alive with thee; they shall be male and
female.

21 And take thou unto thee of all food that is
eaten, and thou shalt gather it to thee; and it
shall be for food for thee and for them.

A self-sufficient ark! And so is Noah destined to confirm
the status quo existent before his adventure. In his actions he
is propelled by the force of imperfectly thought monism -- the
'mythologic' of monism. If he is perfect in his generations, his
generations are very imperfect indeed. Even the Truth about monism is lost on Noah:

(7)

1 And the LORD said unto Noah, come thou and
all thy house into the ark; for thee have I seen
righteous before me in this generation.

'opposition'
(between Noah
and the rest
weakened by the
presence of the
daughters of
men)

2 Of every clean beast thou shalt take to thee
by sevens, the male and his female: and of the
beasts that are not clean by two, the male and
his female.

Separate elements held together in inter-

dependence at Creation now begin to be resolved

into .... annihilation:

'opposition'
(between those
chosen and the
rest weakened by
the presence of
the clean among
the unclean)

4 For yet seven days, and I will cause it to
rain upon the earth forty days and forty nights;
and every living substance that I have made will
I destroy from off the face of the earth.

(Excepting, of course, those within the ark.)

11 the same day were all the fountains of the
great deep broken up, and the windows of heaven
were opened

mediation

12 And the rain was upon the earth forty days
and forty nights.

    ↓ 'opposition'
(between the
elements of

18 And the waters prevailed exceedingly upon
the earth; and all the high hills, that were
under the whole heaven, were covered.

Creation)

The great deep rises to meet Heaven, and Heaven
falls to meet the deep

↓ mediation

23 And every living substance was destroyed
which was upon the face of the ground, both man
and cattle, and the creeping things, and the
fowls of the heaven; and they were destroyed
from the earth: and Noah only remained alive,
and they that were with him in the ark.

↓ "synthesis"
(illusion of
solution)

    The force that had moved them was this: 'opposition' ⟶
weakener ⟶ mediation ⟹ 'synthesis' = the illusion of a solution, achieved by substituting the original opposition between
those chosen and those condemned with a weaker pair and combining
the parties into an artificial unifier, the ark. It is, after
all, a house not a home -- merely a construction unable to exert
any permanent influence on those within.

(8)

    The waters have moved to combine -- but have not united --
to save Noah and his charges from destruction -- the illusion of
synthesis. Hints of a more profound, if flawed, Truth about
life, however, now bring Noah and his ark down to earth. As it
was in the beginning, so too now the waters of Creation separate
and divide:

> 1 and God made a wind to pass over the earth, and
> the waters assuaged;
>
> 2 The fountains also of the deep and the windows
> of heaven were stopped, and the rain from heaven
> was restrained;

> 3   And the waters returned from off the earth con-
> tinually; and after the end of the hundred and
> fifty days the waters were abated.
>
> 4   And the ark rested in the seventh month, on the
> seventeenth day of the month, upon the mountain of
> Ararat.
>
> 13   And it came to pass in the six hundredth and
> first year, in the first month, the first day of
> the month, the waters were dried up from off the
> earth: and Noah removed the covering of the ark,
> and looked, and behold, the face of the ground was
> dry.

In physical space the ark _mediates_ rather than resolves; it comes to rest on a mountain top, _between_ Heaven and earth.   Once back on earth, Noah and his people begin, predictably,   where they had left off before the flood -- in violation of the progressive forces of Creation:

> 20   And Noah builded an altar unto the LORD; and
> took of every clean beast, and of every clean fowl,
> and offered burnt offerings on the altar.

Without the secret of Eden, intelligent life is doomed to destroy intelligent life, despite the best of intentions.   For even intentions are now imprisoned within a monist imagination. God acquiesces in exasperation:

> 21   I will not curse the ground any more for man's
> sake; for the imagination of man's heart is evil
> from his youth.

Even the 'mythologic' of pluralism is now but a shadow. Noah embodies it -- but running in reverse.   There is, first, _separation_ -- of Noah and his family from the rest of humankind, and of certain animals from the rest of animalkind.   This is followed by _opposition_, for example, between Noah's kind and the rest of humankind;   between chosen and unchosen animalkind; between clean and unclean beasts in the ark.   After the flood weakening follows and in the ark there is mediation. Now, there is virtually nothing left of Creation to hold humankind back from its monist course:

(9)

> 1   And God blessed Noah and his sons, and said unto them, Be fruitful, and multiply, and replenish the earth.
>
> 2   And the fear of you and the dread of you shall be upon every beast of the earth, and upon every fowl of the air, upon all that moveth upon the earth, and upon all the fishes of the sea; into your hands are they delivered.
>
> 3   Every moving thing that liveth shall be meat for you; even as the green herb have I given you all things.
>
> 4   But flesh with the life thereof, which is the blood thereof, shall ye not eat.

A 'forbidden fruit', a reminder of life before the fall. All, as Noah's life demonstrates, is not quite forgotten. But it is merely a clue as to a possibility, not a forecast of things to come:

> 5   And surely your blood of your lives will I require; at the hand of every beast will I require it, and at the hand of man; at the hand of every man's brother will I require the life of man.

The future is compounded by violence:

> 6   Whoso sheddeth man's blood, by man shall his blood be shed.

Retribution is a far cry even from complementary opposition. For every action an equal and opposite reaction. Nevertheless, all is not lost. Something still remains of the force for peace:

> 11   And I will establish my covenant with you;
> neither shall all flesh be cut off any more by the
> waters of a flood; neither shall there any more be
> a flood to destroy the earth.

By the same token, neither shall there be a flood to _save_ the best on earth; neither is there any future in proceeding from imperfectly grasped pluralism the 'mythologic' of pluralism -- separation and withdrawal. As a token of God's covenant with humankind a sign is set in nature -- a rainbow connecting heaven and earth. But it is a sign of imperfectly grasped pluralism in another sense, namely, of complementary opposition rather than opposed complementarity. The bow is set in a single element -- the waters -- here appearing in the form of a cloud.

> 13   I do set my bow in the cloud, and it shall be
> for a token of a covenant between me and the earth.

> 16   And the bow shall be in the cloud; and I will
> look upon it, that I may remember the everlasting
> covenant between God and every living creature of
> all flesh that is upon the earth.

And it comes to pass that monism in its extreme form is rejected by Noah:

> 20   And Noah began to be an husbandman, and he
> planted a vinyard:

> 21   And he drank of the wine, and was drunken; and
> he was uncovered within his tent.

> 22   And Ham the father of Canaan, saw the nakedness
> of his father, and told his two brethren without.

> 24   And Noah awoke from his wine, and knew what his
> younger son had done unto him.

> 25   And he said, Cursed be Canaan; a servant of
> servants shall he be unto his bretheren.

Homosexual 'incest' -- oneness reproducing itself into nothingness -- is as untenable a solution as the overthrow of the elder brother by the younger. Ham and his family are banished to a weaker form of incest. Shem and Japheth are allowed a more progressive solution to the problem of survival in isolation -- exchange between two. Fundamentally, though, nothing has changed.

> 26 And he said, Blessed be the LORD God of Shem; and Canaan shall be his servant.
>
> 27 God shall enlarge Japheth, and he shall dwell in the tents of Shem; and Canaan shall be his servant.

Unity, separation, and subordination, mark a confused future.

(10)

Ham and his descendants would people the cities of Babel, Ninevah, Sodom and Gomorrah in the land of Canaan. Shem would come unto the lands of the interior to the east. Japheth and his people would occupy the coastal region.

> 32 These are the families of the sons of Noah, after their generations, in their nations: and by these were the nations divided in the earth after the flood.

But the force prevailing is monism.

(11)

And the whole earth was of one language and one speech. The children of men all gather together in one place determined to merge as one people with one name. They set their own 'bow' in the clouds as a symbol of their 'accomplishment': they raise a tower to Heaven at Babel. But this misrepresents the Truth. And God intervenes to prevent it.

> 6   And the LORD said, Behold, the people is one, and they all have one language; and this they begin to do; and now nothing will be restrained from them, which they have imagined to do.

And the people are moved by the 'mythologic' of pluralism to separate. In their failure, then, lies a hint of success:

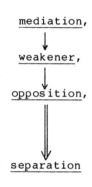

mediation,

weakener,

opposition,

separation

the building of the tower of Babel linking heaven to earth, humankind to God.

God and humankind as similar -- in intelligence and likeness.

God and humankind as different-- inexperience vs. knowledge.

> 7   Go, to, let us go down, and confound their language, that they may not understand one another's speech.

> 8   So the LORD scattered them abroad from thence upon the face of all the earth: and they left off to build the city.

If unity is no solution, neither is separation. But it is closer to the Truth.

(12)

And it comes to pass that Abram is born in the line of Shem; and he takes unto him a wife, Sarai. And Abram is moved to separate from his own lands.

> 5   And Abram took Sarai his wife, and Lot his
> brother's son, and all their substance that they
> had gathered, and the souls that they had gotten in
> Haran; and they went forth to go into the land of
> Canaan; and into the land of Canaan they came.
>
> 6   And Abram passed through the land unto the place
> of Sichem, unto the plain of Moreh.   And the
> Canaanite was in the land.

In lands he occupies, but which are also occupied by others
in superior numbers, the germ of an Idea begins to form in
Abram's head. lands may be held irrespective of occupation if
they are assigned in perpetuity to a continuity of people.

> 7   And the LORD appeared unto Abram, and said, Unto
> thy seed will I give this land: and there builded
> he an altar unto the LORD, who appeared unto him.

But the lands he claims are still occupied by others; and
when famine in on the land, Abram is driven away to Egypt in
search of food.   There he tricks the Pharaoh into an alliance by
offering his wife as a concubine as if she were his sister.   In
return, Pharaoh gives Abram gifts of livestock and servants.   But
Pharaoh's house is beset with great plagues.   The ruse is discovered.   Abram is forced to leave Egypt, but with his possessions intact.   The means to permanent alliances is not yet
apparent.

(13)

So Abram and Lot arrive back in Canaan.   But the land is too
poor to support both their Houses.   Furthermore, the land is also
occupied by the Canaanites and the Perizzites.   The technological
development which might see them through to self-sufficiency despite the resource-population-alien problem has not yet material-
ized and the old social relations of production bequeathing

inheritance to the first-born still persist. The two brothers agree to separate and Lot leaves.

> 8 And Abram said unto Lot, Let there be no strife,
> I pray thee between me and thee, and between my
> herdmen and thy herdmen; for we be brethren.
>
> 9 Is not the whole land before thee? separate
> thyself, I pray thee, from me: if thou wilt take
> the left hand, then I will go to the right; or if
> thou depart to the right hand, then I will go to
> the left.
>
> 11 Then Lot chose him all the plain of Jordan:
> and Lot journeyed east: and they separated
> themselves the one from the other.
>
> 12 Abram dwelled in the land of Canaan, and Lot
> dwelled in the cities of the plain, and pitched his
> tent toward Sodom.

Now the Idea comes more clearly than ever to Abram.

> 14 And the LORD said unto Abram, after that Lot
> was separated from him, Lift up now thine eyes, and
> look from the place where thou art northward, and
> southward, and eastward, and westward:
>
> 15 For all the land which thou seest, to thee will
> I give it, and to thy seed for ever.

* * * * *

The Idea continues to grow.

> 17.8 And I will give unto thee, and to thy seed
> after thee, the land wherein thou art a stranger,
> all the land of Canaan, for an everlasting posses-
> sion; and I will be their God.

For his accomplishments, Abram's name becomes Abraham. But the land is still occupied by strangers and violence and bloodshed reign over it. In the absence of respect for his claims, Abraham will have to secure temporal possession of Canaan eliminating potential rivals even amongst his own people. Sodom and Gomorrah are destroyed and Lot is condemned to an incestuous relationship with his own daughters.

Abraham now withdraws to Gerar where he tries to trick the king, Abimalech, into an alliance through his wife as he had done with the Egyptians. But he is discovered before Abimalech consumates the relationship. Now Abimalech offers Abraham an alliance of brotherhood. Abraham accepts. With this success follows Abraham's first peaceful acquisition of land in Canaan. He purchases land in Hebron within which to bury his wife, now named Sarah, who has died there. Her purpose has been fulfilled with the birth of a son, Isaac.

> 23.2 And Sarah died in Kirjatharba; the same is Hebron in the land of Canaan: and Abraham came to mourn for Sarah, and to weep for her.
>
> 3 And Abraham stood up from before his dead, and spake unto the sons of Heth saying,
>
> 4 I am a stranger and a sojourner with you: give me possessions of a burying place with you, that I may bury my dead out of my sight.

But the children of Heth would prefer merely to let Abraham use the land, and not sign away their title. But finally a deal is struck. There is no doubt that Abraham is on the right track: a death, anti-thesis, heralds into being the practice = thesis of the Idea. The relationship of Abraham's people to Heth's in consequence, however, remains uncertain.

Then follows another successful alliance, this one through a marriage between Abraham's son Isaac and Rebekah, daughter of

Bethuel of Mesopotamia. Abraham's purpose has been fulfilled --
a fraternal and a marriage alliance for his people and successful
acquisition of parts of the promised land. He dies and is buried
alongside Sarah, making doubly sure of the lands they have bought
by also 'occupying' them.

And Isaac begets Esau and Jacob who now take up the old
struggle between the technical means of production and the social
relations of production, left in abeyance since the time of Cain
and Abel. Nature suggests a solution: Esau and Jacob are twins;
there is no first-born. But culture dictates otherwise so that
the first to emerge from the womb will inherit, and that is Esau.

> 25.27 And the boys grew: and Esau was a cunning
> hunter, a man of the field; and Jacob was a plain
> man dwelling in tents.

The elder brother inherits the earlier technology -- hunting
-- in fact the earliest technology. The younger inherits the
most advanced -- herding. It is the hunter, then, who will become the leader of his people, whose seed will continue the line
of authority. The technical development represented by Jacob
will therefore be impeded, and this is not in the interests of
self-sufficiency on the land.

Esau's skills fail in time of crisis. He is overcome by the
heat and nearly dies of exhaustion. But he comes upon Jacob in
the field and Jacob exploits the situation to acquire Esau's
birthright in exchange for saving his life:

> :32 And Esau said, Behold I am at the point to
> die: and what profit shall this birthright do to
> me?

> :33 And Jacob said, Swear to me this day; and he
> sware unto him: and he sold his birthright unto
> Jacob.

> :34 Then Jacob gave Esau bread and pottage of len-
> tils; and he did eat and drink, and rose up, and
> went his way.

Hunting and herding are now in Jacob's possession. All that
is required now is that he usurp Esau's position as Isaac's successor for the solution to be complete. But the event also
points out the weakness of a previous solution -- how precarious
an everlasting possession that can be bought, sold or bartered!

There is famine in the land and Isaac travels to Gerar where
his father had made allies before him. But the alliance has died
with his father. He is forced to trick the locals, as his father
had done, into thinking his wife Rebekah was his sister so that
she will be taken into the King's household as a concubine. But
the new King Abimalech also discovers the ruse and, like his
father, allows Isaac to dwell in peace amongst them.

And Isaac prospers exceedingly, so much so that Abimalech
begins to fear for his own power. He sends Isaac away to the
valley of Gerar where his father had been before him. There
Isaac uncovers the wells dug by his father, but the local inhabitants of that country force Isaac away. It appears that continuity of labour in the land is not sufficient to establish a
prior claim. Force of occupation again wins out. Isaac is now
moved to issue forth his God-given right to the lands of Abimalech; Abimalech reconsiders his position and offers Isaac a renew-
al of the old alliance:

> 26:28 And they said, We saw certainly that the
> LORD was with thee: and we said, Let there be now
> an oath betwixt us, even betwixt us and thee, and
> let us make a covenant with thee.
>
> :29 That thou wilt do us no hurt, as we have not
> touched thee, and as we have done unto thee nothing
> but good and have sent thee away in peace.

It is now that Jacob conspires with his mother to resolve
the inheritance/technology problem by acquiring Esau's birth-

right.   In this way the old social relations of production will
be overthrown and the way paved for technological progress.

Isaac is nearing death and he instructs his son Esau to hunt
deer in the fields and bring him venison as savoury meat, that he
may eat of it and bless Jacob as his successor.   But Rebekah
overhears the conversation and summons Jacob.   He must bring two
kids from his flock which she will prepare as savoury meat for
his father.   Isaac's eyes are failing; Jacob disguised as Esau
might well receive the blessing intended for his brother and so
acquire his inheritence.   So Rebekah dresses Jacob in Esau's
clothes and covers his hands and neck with goat's hair to make
him rough to the touch as is his brother.   And Isaac knows him
not and blesses him.

> 27:29   Let people serve thee, and nations bow down
> to thee: be lord over thy bretheren, and let thy
> mother's sons bow down to thee: cursed be everyone
> that curseth thee, and blessed be he that blesseth
> thee.

When Esau finally appears with his venison, he and his
father realize what has happened.   But a blessing bestowed must
stand.   Esau's delay has demonstrated conclusively the inferi-
ority of hunting over herding.   But it shall come to pass that
Esau will eventually emerge superior over his brother.

> 27:40   And by the sword shalt thou live, and shalt
> serve thy brother; and it shall come to pass when
> thou shalt have the dominion, that thou shalt break
> his yoke from off thy neck.

This solution promises bloodshed and Isaac is forced to
separate the brothers.   He sends Jacob to Padanaram in Mesopotamia to find a wife.   He will not return for 20 years.

Jacob finally makes his way back to Canaan with his wives
Laban and Rachel.   In anticipation of his arrival Esau sets out
to meet him with a force of 400 men.   Jacob fears for his life

and so he divides his household into two parts lest one and all
be destroyed. Unwittingly he has moved according to the force of
pluralism: anti-thesis ──➤ thesis, but reaches a mythological
conclusion = separation-withdrawal.   Esau moves to correct the
error: he has come out to welcome, not to destroy, his brother.
Jacob's trickery must be forgiven in the interest of progress,
but the brothers are unsure of their own conclusion. The two are
not yet moved by the force that moves the one.

Esau refuses Jacob's gifts and accepts instead his blessing.
Jacob declines to leave some of his people with Esau as a token
of their new relationship. Each sees the gesture as unnecessary
given their reconciliation, but in truth both are still unsure of
their future relationship.

However, the anti-thesis necessary to reform their relationship is moving in the world around them. The question is, would
it move them before it destroyed them?

Dinah, Jacob's daughter, is abducted and raped by the prince
of the Havites; but the prince falls in love with her and desires
her also as wife. To the Havites, this 'alliance' will merely be
the prelude to the absorption of Jacob's people and their possessions:

> 34:23 Shall not their cattle and their substance
> and every beast of their's be our's? only let us
> consent unto them and they will dwell with us.

On the pretext of accepting the offer of alliance, Jacob's
sons plot their sister's revenge.

> :14 And they said unto them, We cannot do this
> thing, to give our sister to one that is uncircum-
> cized: for that were a reproach unto us:
>
> :15 But in this will we consent unto you: if ye
> will be as we be, that every male of you be circum-
> cized.

:16   Then we will give our daughters unto you, and
we will take your daughters unto us, and we will
dwell with you, and we will become one people.

This is precisely what the Havites have in mind; and they
agree.   But after they have been circumcized and are off their
guard, Dinah's brothers, Simeon and Levi, enter the Havite city
and slay all the males.   In so doing they not only avenge their
sister but also eliminate a rival people whose lands in Canaan
they claim as their own.   But the countryside is roused against
them:

anti-thesis

:30   And Jacob said to Simeon and Levi, Ye have
troubled me to make me stink among the inhabitants
of the land, among the Canaanites and Perizzites:
and I being few in number, they shall gather
themselves together against me, and slay me; and I
shall be destroyed, I and my house.

thesis

At Bethel, the solution strikes him, as it had struck his
grandfather before him: inalienable, eternal jurisdiction over
the land:

35:12   And the land which I gave Abraham and Isaac,
to thee I will give it, and to thy seed after thee
will I give the land.

And so was Jacob's name changed to Israel.   But how was the
solution to be achieved?

Jacob returns to his brother Esau, but the lands within which they dwell cannot support them, so they part. Esau comes to found the kingdom of Edom to the south-east and Jacob once more comes to live amongst strangers in Canaan.

(37)

And Jacob's seventh born is Joseph, first born to Rachel, Jacob's second wife, but first of his choice. And Joseph has a dream:

> 7   For, behold, we were binding sheaves in the field, and, lo my sheaf arose, and also stood up-right; and behold, your sheaves stood round about, and made obeisance to my sheaf.
>
> 8   And his brethren said unto him, Shalt thou in-deed reign over us? or shalt thou indeed have dominion over us? And they hated him yet the more for his dream, and for his words,

For Joseph is not the first born, destined to succeed; and yet his father loves him above all the rest. Then Joseph dreams another dream:

> 9   behold, the sun and the moon and the eleven stars made obeisance to me.
>
> 10 And he told it to his father, and to his breth-ren: and his father rebuked him, and said unto him, What is this dream that thou hast dreamed? Shall I and thy mother and thy brethren indeed come to bow down ourselves to thee to the earth?

Would the son become even greater than the father in his own lifetime? Would neither the eldest nor the youngest -- Benjamin -- succeed? Would the problem of the old social relations of production and new technological possibilities be resolved by a middle-of-the-road succession or even by a complete overthrow of the system? Joseph's brethren decide not -- they conspire to kill him.

But Reuben the eldest and Jacob's successor intervenes to prevent them. Judah, Joseph's younger brother, persuades the bretheren to sell Joseph into bondage to the Ishmaelites. And so comes Joseph into Egypt, into the household of Potiphar, captain of the guard in the service of Pharoah.

In the end, separation -- the outcome of Reuben's attempt to mediate and weaken his brothers' resolve to murder (anti-thesis) Joseph. A potential now emerges for movement along the path of imperfectly thought pluralism and the stage is set for another major cycle of Israelite history: separation $\longrightarrow$ mediation $\longrightarrow$ weakener $\longrightarrow$ opposition $\Longrightarrow$ separation-withdrawal. Certainly it must see the status quo confirmed but with the experience of at least imperfectly thought pluralism continuing on through into the future.

Judah, the initiator of this scenario, sums up the utter futility of the Israelites' situation. It is his fate to be tricked into incest with his daughter Tamar and she bears him twins whose first-born status is impossible to determine even with the first-out-of-the-womb rule in place:

> 28: And it came to pass, when she travelled, that the one put out his hand: and the midwife took and bound upon his hand a scarlet thread, saying, This came out first.

> 29: And it came to pass, as he drew back his hand, that behold, his brother came out: and she said, How hast thou broken forth?

The Jews will remain an enclave out of necessity while searching solutions to unsolvable problems of their own creation.

(39)

Potiphar's house prospers with Joseph's arrival and Joseph becomes its overseer. But he refuses to assimilate to Egyptian society. He rebuffs the advances of Potiphar's wife who seeks her revenge by falsely accusing him. Potiphar banishes him to prison.

(40)

And it comes to pass that Pharaoh's butler and baker are imprisoned with Joseph. And the butler dreams a dream which he relates to Joseph: there appeared a vine with three branches, and the branches brought forth many grapes. These the butler pressed into wine and offered to his master. "Within three days you will be restored to your position," says Joseph.

And the baker too has a dream: on his head were piled three baskets and in the uppermost were bakemeats for Pharaoh. But the birds ate the bakemeats leaving him with nothing. "Within three days you will be delivered up from prison and hanged," says Joseph.

And it is as Joseph foretells: the nonproducer who had brought forth abundance is restored and the producer who had wasted all through carelessness is hanged.

(41)

And Pharaoh dreams a dream that his priests cannot interpret. The butler remembers Joseph and tells Pharaoh.

> 17 And the Pharaoh said unto Joseph, In my dream, behold, I stood upon the bank of the river:
>
> 18 And behold, there came up out of the river seven kine, fatfleshed and well favoured; and they fed in a meadow:

19   And, behold, seven other kine came up after
them, poor and very ill favoured and lean fleshed,
such as I never saw in all the land of Egypt for
badness:

20   And the lean and the ill favoured kine did eat
up the first seven fat kine:

21   And when they had eaten them up, it could not
be known that they had eaten them; but they were
still ill favoured as at the beginning.   So I
awoke.

And the dream repeats itself with stalks of corn -- first
full and then thin ears.   These two dreams are one says Joseph:

29   Behold, there come seven years of great plenty
throughout all the land of Egypt:

30   And there shall arise after them seven years of
famine; and all the plenty shall be forgotten in
the land of Egypt; and the famine shall consume the
land.

Joseph advises Pharaoh to appoint an overseer to gather
together a fifth part of the produce of Egypt during the plente-
ous years and store it against the famine years to come.   And
Pharaoh does as he advises and appoints Joseph as administrator.

40   only in the throne will I be greater than thou.

The alliance is cemented by the marriage of Joseph to an
Egyptian woman who bears him two sons.   Joseph now stands as a
potential mediator between the Egyptians and the Israelites.   In
his new position he stands well positioned to weaken resolve on
both sides: the Egyptians' to subjugate the peoples of Canaan,
the Israelites to suffer alone in isolation and be torn asunder
by their own internal problems.

For Joseph has now inherited a new technology -- he is
administrator over the irrigated agricultural system of Egypt.
He has become a planner. But he has accomplished it **without**
contravening the old Israelite social relations of production.
While primogeniture remains in force at home in Canaan, in Egypt
Joseph is a 'guest', bound neither by Israelite custom, nor Egyptian. Ability alone wins him through. Joseph is there to be
grasped as a solution, **if** the Israelites want him.

> 56 And the famine was over the face of the earth;
> and Joseph opened all the storehouses, and sold
> unto the Egyptians; and the famine waxed sore in
> the land of Egypt.

> 57 And all countries came into Egypt to Joseph for
> to buy corn; Because that the famine was so sore
> in all the lands.

To the Israelites famine was **anti-thesis** for they had nowhere else to go outside their lands.

(42)

> 3 And Joseph's ten brethren went down to buy corn
> in Egypt.

> 4 But Benjamin, Joseph's brother, Jacob sent not
> with his brethren; for he said, Lest peradventure
> mischief befall him.

> 8 And Joseph knew his brethren, but they knew him
> not.

> 9 And Joseph remembered the dream which he   opposition
> dreamed of them, and said unto them, Ye are
> spies; to see the nakedness of the land ye   ↓
> are come.

> 19 If ye be true men, let one of your   weakening
> bretheren be bound in the house of your   (spies would
> prison; go ye, carry corn for the famine of   not leave
> your houses: hostages)

> 20 But bring your youngest brother unto
> me; so shall your words be verified.   ↓

24 And he turned himself about from them, and wept; and returned to them again, and communed with them, and took from them Simeon, and bound him before their eyes.

25 Then Joseph commanded to fill their sacks with corn, and to restore every man's money into his sack, and to give them provisions for the way: and thus did he unto them.

26 And they came unto Jacob their Father unto the land of Canaan, and told him all that befell unto them;

weakening (despots would not give gifts to their subjects)

But Jacob will not allow his sons to take Benjamin back to Egypt.

(43)

Famine continues within the land of Canaan so that, soon, all the stores the brothers had brought from Egypt are depleted.

11 And their father Israel said unto them, if it must be so now, do this: take of the best fruits in the land in your vessels, and carry down the man a present,

12 And take double money in your hand; and the money that was brought again in the mouth of your sacks, carry it again in your hand; adventure it was an oversight.

13 Take also your brother, and arise, go again unto the man.

And they do: but Joseph refuses to accept the money and instead takes their gifts and releases their brother Simeon. Joseph's role as mediator between Egypt and Israel now begins.

16   And when Joseph saw Benjamin with
them, he said to the ruler of his
house, Bring these men home, and slay,
and make ready; for these men shall
dine with me at noon.

mediation   32   And they set on for him by himself, and for them by themselves, and
for the Egyptians, which did not eat
with him, by themselves: because the
Egyptians might not eat bread with the
Hebrews; for that is an abomination
unto the Egyptians.

(44)

Joseph once again orders his stewards
to fill his brothers' sack with grain
and return the money they had spent.
In Benjamin's sack they place a silver
goblet.

And when the Israelites go forth to
Canaan, they are pursued by Joseph's
servants.   And the servants untie
Benjamin's sack and find the goblet
which belongs to Joseph.   And the
brothers are forced to return to
Egypt.

Judah, who had sold Joseph into bondage, says unto his brother whom he
knows not:

27   And thy servant my father said
unto us, Ye know that my wife bare me
two sons:

28   And the one went out from me, and
I said, Surely he is torn in pieces;
and I saw him not since:

29 And if ye take this also from me,
and mischief befall him, ye shall
bring down my gray hairs with sorrow
to the grave.

33 Now therefore, I pray thee, let
thy servant abide instead of the lad a
bondman to my lord; and let the lad go
up with his bretheren.

34 For how shall I go up to my fa-   mediation
ther, and the lad be not with me?
lest peradventure I see the evil that
shall come on my father.

Judah, who separated father from son,

now moves to reunite them.

(45)

Then Joseph could not refrain himself

before all them that stood by him; and

he cried, Cause every man to go out

from me. And there stood no man with

him, while Joseph made himself known

unto his bretheren.

5 Now therefore be not grieved, nor
angry with yourselves, that ye sold me
hither: for God did send me before
you to preserve life.

9 Haste ye, and go up to my father,
and say unto him, Thus said thy son
Joseph, God hath made me lord of all
Egypt: come down unto me, tarry not:

26 And Jacob's heart fainted, for he
believed them not.

27 And they told him all the words of
Joseph, which he had said unto them:
and when he saw the wagons which
Joseph had sent to carry him, the spirit of Jacob their father revived:

28 And Israel said, It is enough I   synthesis
will go see him before I die.

But Joseph's reconciliation with his father and
brethren unfolded according to the 'mythologic' of
monism. <u>Illusion</u> moved his brothers to expel him to
Egypt -- the illusion that this solution would be as
final as his death. But, as Reuben 'realized',
Joseph and his brethren were not truly opposed -- the
succession versus development problem would remain no
matter what fate befell him. And Reuben moved his
brothers to moderate their intentions. In the end,
Joseph offers not a solution to the Israelites'
internal and external problems, but merely a
reprieve. He offers them life but with something
worse than the old <u>status quo</u>: The Israelites are
now completely removed from their Promised Lands in
Canaan with not even the right of occupation to justify their claims. Meanwhile Joseph continues in his
role as mediator between the Israelites and the Egyptians.

16 And the fame thereof was heard in Joseph's house,
saying Joseph's brethren are come: and it pleased
Pharaoh well, and his servants.

(46)

And so, surrounded by enemies and in the midst of
famine the Israelites leave Canaan: <u>anti-thesis</u> --
but the Idea continues.

3 And he said, I am God, the God of thy father:
fear not to go down into Egypt; for I will make of
thee a great nation:

4 I will go down with thee into Egypt; and I will
also surely bring thee up again:

29 And Joseph made ready his chariot, and went up to
meet Israel his father, to Goshen, and presented himself unto him; and he fell on his neck and wept a
good while.

(47)

THEN Joseph came and told Pharaoh, and said, My
father and my brethren, and their flocks, and their
herds, and all that they have, are come out of the
land of Canaan; and, behold, they are in the land of
Goshen.

weakening
(of Israel-
ites as mere-
ly residents
in the land
of Egypt)

4   They said moreover unto Pharaoh, For to sojourn
in the land we are come; for thy servants have no
pasture for their flocks; for the famine is sore
in the land of Canaan; now therefore, we pray
thee, let thy servants dwell in the land of
Goshen.

5   And the Pharaoh spake unto Joseph, saying, Thy
father and thy brethren are come unto thee:

weakening
(of Egyptians
as absolute
rulers in
their lands)

6   The land of Egypt is before thee; in the best
of the land make thy father and thy brethren to
dwell; in the land of Goshen let them dwell: and
if thou knowest any men of activity among them,
then make them rulers over my cattle.

But Joseph gives his people not just residence but
possession in the land:

opposition
(with Egypt
now poten-
tial)

11 And Joseph placed his father and his brether-
en, and gave them a possession in the land of
Egypt, in the best of the land, in the land of
Rameses, as Pharaoh had commanded.

The seven years of famine that Joseph had predict-
ed come to pass. And the people of Egypt suffer exceedingly. Soon they have used all their money to
pay for the stores of grain that Joseph has pre-
pared. Then they are forced to sell their livestock
and finally their lands for to buy food. And all
their property is rendered unto Pharaoh by Joseph.

Only the Egyptian priests and the Israelites remain unaffected, for the priests are subsidized by

Pharaoh and the Israelites hold possession in the best part of the land with Joseph as their protector.

Finally, lest the Egyptian people starve, Joseph distributes seed amongst them on condition that a fifth part of the yield should go to Pharaoh and four-fifths to themselves for subsistence. The subjugation of the people to the Pharaoh is now complete. And herein again lies a message for the Israelites: without inalienable tenure, with alienable private property in the land and resources, their future will be precarious indeed. In a free market situation, crisis breeds bankruptcy, and bankruptcy means surrendering one's birthright to monopoly if life is to be maintained. Monopoly, in turn, breeds despotism. The irony is that the agent of this oppression is the Israelite Joseph -- merely 'doing his job' amongst the Egyptians to show his own people the way.

27   And Israel dwelt in the land of Egypt, in the country of Goshen; and they had possessions therein, and grew, and multiplied exceedingly.

(48)

Israel's time had come:

3   And Jacob said unto Joseph, God Almighty appeared to me at Luz in the land of Canaan, and blessed me,

4   And said unto me, Behold, I will make thee fruitful and multiply thee, and I will make of thee a multitude of people; and will give this land to thy seed after thee for an everlasting possession.

And Israel blesses the sons of Joseph, placing his right hand on the youngest and his left on the eldest. This greatly puzzles Joseph, for his father has thereby decreed that the youngest will succeed. This would overthrow the old Israelite social relations of production. Thus is the possibility of technological innovation released. But gone is the authority of accumulated wisdom to guide the future. But this 'solution' is for Joseph's line only. Of what failure is he guilty to deserve this?

(49)

Joseph, in fact, is moved by the force of imperfectly grasped pluralism. As such he can achieve a temporary accommodation with the Egyptians but he cannot transcend the problem that the Israelites now face, merely occupation of land in Egypt which the Egyptians claim as their own: not even occupation of land they claim in Canaan which others now occupy. All Joseph has done is bought time for Israel so that they can regroup for another assault on the fortresses of Canaan.

However, in the process Joseph has discovered a new means, one that heralds a far more progressive future. He has grasped something of the real historical circumstances in which the Israelites now find themselves: anti-thesis $\longrightarrow$ thesis. He heralds a far more progressive future whose final term cannot yet be identified. Plurality, opposed complementary, remain but a shadow hidden in symbol.

22 Joseph is a fruitful bough, even a fruitful bough by a well; whose branches run over the wall:

25 Even by the God of thy father, who shall help thee; and by the Almighty, who shall bless thee with blessings of heaven above, blessings of the deep that lieth under, blessings of the breasts, and of the womb.

26   The blessings of thy father have prevailed above
the blessings of my progenitors unto the utmost bound
of the everlasting hills: they shall be on the head
of Joseph, and on the crown of the head of him that
was separated from his brethren.

Joseph's failure is that he merely points the way.

Israel grasps the implications sufficiently to see
that a complete transcendence of the Israelite problem of inheritance versus technological progress is
necessary.

He blesses as his own successor, neither the eldest nor the youngest, but qualities characteristic
of each of his sons.   The future requires,

        the violence of a Simeon and a Levi,

        the authority and wisdom of a Judah,

        the might of a Reuben,

        the cunning of a Dan,

        the labour of an Isachar,

        the perseverence of a Gad,

        the technical competence of an Asher,

        the bartering skills of a Zebulum,

        the oratory of a Zilpah.

which all add up to the future of a Benjamin.

27   Benjamin shall ravin as a wolf: in the morning
he shall devour the prey, and at night he shall divide the spoil.

At best, complementary opposition.

The blessings of heaven and the deep, though, rest
with Joseph.

(50)

And Israel dies

And Joseph dies

anti-thesis

↓

Who or what will save the Israelites now?

↓

(1)

Weakeners removed, the oppositions they subordinate are now released:

8 Now there arose up a new king over Egypt, which knew not Joseph

9 And he said unto his people, Behold, the people of the children of Israel are more and mightier than we:

thesis
(Egyptian sovereignty)

↓

opposition

10 Come on, let us deal wisely with them; lest they multiply, and it come to pass, that, when there falleth out any war, they join also unto our enemies, and fight against us, and so get them up out of the land.

anti-thesis
(Israelite power in Egypt)

↓

11 Therefore did they set over them taskmasters to afflict them with their burdens.

synthesis
(Egyptian subordination of Israel)

separation-withdrawal
(of the Israelites from their possessions and from the Egyptians as a people and a class)

14 And they made their lives bitter with hard bondage, in mortar, and in brick, and in all manner of service in the field; all their services, wherein they made them serve, was with rigour.

And still the Israelites multiply.

And the Pharaoh orders more extreme measures to be taken:

↓

15   And the king of Egypt spake to the
Hebrew midwives,

16   And he said, When ye do the office
of a midwife to the Hebrew women, and
see them upon the stools; if it be a
son, then ye shall kill him: but if
it be a daughter, then she shall live.

The Hebrew midwives deceive Pharaoh, saying that the Hebrew women bear
their children before the midwives
reach them.

22   And Pharaoh charged all his
people, saying every son that is born
ye shall cast into the river, and
every daughter ye shall save alive.

Driven from Canaan by famine, surrounded by hostile tribes, torn by
internal problems, dispossessed by
Egypt. Now genocide. The Israelites
are as nothing. But history is once
more on their side, if they can but
survive their own destruction.

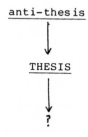

anti-thesis

THESIS

?

With Eden as our point of reference, this reading reveals there the outlines of a particular way of life and the process of its coming into being. We find five seemingly resource-specific countries aligned along a river as water-giver to mineral-taker. Then there's Eden's 'forbidden fruits' and food taboos thereafter -- species that the members of the country must not consume. There's also 'forbidden love', a prohibition on 'marriage between members of the same country'.

We immediately see in this the outlines of the Australian Aboriginal way of life -- kinline-confederation: "clan" linkage and economic interdependence; totemic prohibitions; "clan" exogamy. And there is more: Adam and Eve are moved out of the Garden by an Australian quality of thought which concludes, 'separate and withdraw'. Woman in Eden is as much a force against oneness as a force for -- as sister woman is an agent of federation between "clans". Women's lot to suffer the pain of childbirth as punishment for sin can be seen as a metaphor for the new course on which Adam and Eve have embarked whereby the woman actually becomes the mother of her own children in culture as well as nature. In Australia the woman is merely the receptacle within which the moulding of the child takes place while the father, through 'moulding', provides its spiritual or "clan" identity; the woman's own children are actually those of her brother. (By contrast, in incorporative, Cree society, both husband and wife are 'parents' to 'their' children.) Finally, land in Eden, or at least in the attempt to regain Eden thereafter, is abstract, eternal jurisdiction -- a Promised Land -- whereas with the Australians it is Dreamtime substance, in both cases once and for all in the beginning in its association with a particular continuity of people.

The Australian symbolic archetype, line, bars any return to Eden in the form of a flaming sword. Line predictably begins to

give way to circle -- the archetype of incorporation -- as Eden
recedes from view. For instance, there's the rainbow, a semicircle, as a sign of God's covenant with humankind. In this connection we understand why the serpent is chosen to symbolize the
'choice' posed humankind in Eden: the serpent is neither line
nor circle/both line and circle depending on how he sets himself.

There are, however, some anomalies as far as the Australian
parallel is concerned. Life in Eden exists in respect of
Creation; its intelligent life forms live in respect of each
other. But the Australians were hunters as well as gatherers --
meat eaters. Perhaps Genesis is alluding to a time past when
complementarity was without opposition even in a subordinate
capacity. Then again, perhaps the proscriptions are an imagina-
tive construct, a hope for things to come.

In the beginning was One, the waters from which the plurality of heaven and earth emerged. One is unity, synthesis, incorporation. The process culminating in Eden is, of course,
emergence out of this: anti-thesis $\longrightarrow$ thesis $\Longrightarrow$ complementarity. It is familiar to use us as an offshoot of the monist
historical process. Translated in 'Australian' terms what it
suggests is this: in response to the predatory designs of an
ego-oriented, incorporating people (anti-thesis), others, in
order to preserve their respective integrities intact (thesis),
move to accommodate one to the other through invention of and
mutual respect for one another's jurisdiction (complementarity).
The one arrangement -- the Creator One -- we have termed 'locality-incorporative', the other -- the derivative Two -- 'kinline
confederation'. And as we have seen, the Creator One is really a
scattering of Ones, each situated independently of the rest and
each regarding itself as the universe.

But what justifies this extrapolation from a story about
physical Creation to an historical process? Alien-others in the

kind of incorporating society that is our point of departure here
are generally represented as non-human, as in the story of Iyas.
The more alien they are the less human and more animal-like they
become.   If distant humans why not distant events, the events
themselves becoming progressively naturalized the more remote
they are from the present?   If we take Genesis as a statement
about ultimate origins then -- the claim it makes for itself --
what is recorded here is the origins not of the Australians but
of kinline-confederation as a system.

Now kinline-confederation, with its Idea of abstract, eternal jurisdiction over, through and below land or territory (i.e.,
locality) must surely have required a fully-developed human cognitive capacity as a prerequisite for its creation.   For only
this would allow a grasping of the abstract Idea as such.   In
fact, the development might even have required an intelligence
higher than our own considering the difficulties we have had in
grasping the nature of the Australians' accomplishments.   Either
we are not up to the Australians' cranial capacities or we are in
a 'locality-incorporative' phase of our own which blinds us to
the alternative possibility, particularly in others.   In the
interests of our own peace of mind though, we would be well
advised to accept the second hypothesis: the human race, then,
is uniformly homo sapiens sapiens. We all share the same ability
for abstract thought.   'We' are as capable of a 'kinline-confederational' phase as 'they' are.

What I, Genesis, seem to be implying here is that locality-
incorporation as a way of life is the more primitive form.   And
in hunter-gatherer studies it must be admitted that some anthropologists have gone out of their way to make it seem so.   This is
Swartz and Jordan writing in their textbook, Anthropology:

> The open communities of chimpanzees and the other
> great apes resemble at least some contemporary

hunting and gathering groups in a number of respects. Societies such as the northwestern Atha-
paskan Indians, the Great Basin Shoshoni of the
Southwest, several Eskimo groups, and the Hadze of
Tanzania (in East Africa) have nuclear families as
their basic units and form larger groupings on a
temporary and casual basis. The largest group is a
regional one like the chimpanzee open community,
and a smaller, family group is the most stable and
permanent component of the larger group. Great
flexibility exists in these hunting and gathering
societies, and individuals and nuclear families
come together and separate as food supplies require
and make possible. The individuals and families
use ties of kinship as a basis for combination.
They have siblings and other kin living in different parts of a wide territory, which gives them
ties assuring them and their families of a welcome
in an area where food conditions may be more
favourable than the ones in the area where they had
been living.

But Swartz and Jordan -- and those on whom they have relied
for 'data' -- do the Athapaskans, the Great Basin Shoshoni, the
Eskimo, the Hadza and others who have been likewise 'described',
like the Cree, a great disservice. For what they do is neglect
incorporation in favour of locality in assessing the state of
their societies. And what incorporation is, is a cultural process translating potentially hostile 'outsiders' into 'insiders'
through co-production association. Indeed, it is co-production
association not locality as such -- let alone kinship -- that
defines basic relations in these societies.

Assuming that my findings are generally valid and that these
anthropologists are at least of average intelligence, the explanation must be that they are reading aspects of their own society
into those of other peoples. This, again, raises some interesting questions about the nature of their own society.

Locality-incorporation was also a human achievement requir-
ing an abstract intelligence equal to our own. And while in a
sense an evolutionary precursor, as theory and Genesis point out,

it is a recurring evolutionary precursor, with laws intrinsic to
its own nature and its own subsequent elaborations. This brings
us to the issue of 'the fall' in Genesis.

A particular stream of history (monism), a way of life
(akin to locality-incorporation), re-emerged in Eden and came to
predominate. As it did, pluralism (kinline-confederation),
receded into the background persisting for a time as a mode of
thought, then as a collection of signs, and finally as the Idea
of a Promised Land (but only one amongst what should have been
many). This fall into singularity is marked by the consumption
of a forbidden fruit signifying the union of Garden and people,
not to mention of the people themselves. Eve's 'return gift'
which would have effected perfect complementarity (a part of the
other in the one and vice versa without loss of integrity of
either, something which Genesis never does accomplish) is therefore flawed. Instead, something of the same element is placed in
both, a mistaken notion of complementarity, indeed, one carrying
imperialist overtones. Genesis specifies the process of this
fall on two planes, 1) theoretical: thesis $\longrightarrow$ anti-thesis $\Longrightarrow$;
2) historical: one withdrew from the five to pursue autonomy and
self-determination in a new Promised Land all its own. Intruig-
ingly, 'five into four won't go', is actually a recorded scenario
in the Australian ethnographic record.

As we have seen, the Australian systems operate basically on
an even-numbered basis from a base of two or a base of four
"clans". In the base-two Kariera arrangement the ideal is direct
exchange in marriage between the same two "clans" in consecutive
generations, each "clan" being totemically linked to others in
its own exclusive company of "clans". In the base four Aranda
system the ideal is direct exchange between the same two "clans"
in alternate generations, each of the resulting four "clans" it
takes to make a system being linked to others in its own exclusive company of "clans".

Five "clans", then, is an impossible number with which to
operate a system. Five is the number of estates specified in
Genesis. One would have to go.

In Australia there was often an odd "clan" out in circumstances where a base-two society was in the process of changing to a base-four or vice versa: The vice versa we have already dealt with in the discussion of the Aranda→Kariera transition.

Imagine now, if you will, a perfect world in which two "clans" consistently intermarry from generation to generation in Kariera fashion: A with B. One set of totemic ties link A to "clans" C, D and E in the world outside; another set of ties link B to F, G, and H, and elsewhere. Suppose A journeys to the estate of "clan" C where they find D and E have also congregated to celebrate the travels of their totemic federator. Here they discover that one of them, E, has learned of new truths about the totem's travels. Instead of there being but one journey linking them all, in fact there were two by two different beings -- one linking "clans" A and C, the other D and E. Or so E's neighbours to the west who practice alternate generation exchange, Aranda prescriptions, have convinced E. A is now also persuaded. What it means is that A must now distinguish the mother's mother's "clan" from their own as the mother-in-law "clan". This, in turn, implies that marriage with a person whose mother is in one's own "clan" should be forbidden. A returns home.

B -- A's traditional marriage partner -- however, still recognizes the existence of but one totemic track on its side and but one on A's, as well as the Kariera marriage system that goes along with it, that is, exchange with the same "clan", A, in consecutive generations. A, though, can now only give spouses to B without taking any back in return, for to do so would mean marrying someone with a mother in one's own "clan". And A is hardly likely to give without even the prospect of receiving. As Marcel Mauss points out in The Gift, the whole point of giving is to impose an obligation to reciprocate on the part of the receiver. Alternatively, A may abandon B as a marriage partner and look to other "clans" in the area who have also become more Aranda-like. B, on the other hand, may now find themselves surrounded by nothing but Aranda-like peoples -- nothing but emerging 'fours'.

And five into four won't go. <u>B</u> may be forced to move elsewhere <u>or</u> they may decide to go it alone as a self-reproducing "clan".

Of course, it would hardly ever come to that. It is too easy for <u>B</u> to become 'persuaded' of the new Aranda arrangement for the simple reason that it has no adaptive disadvantages relative to the Kariera. It is unlikely that a whole region would change at the same rate and therefore there are likely to be other Kariera around with whom <u>B</u> can deal. Totemic ties to other "clans" would still exist to provide <u>B</u> with a place amongst its companions and their Kariera partners elsewhere. But isolation and a move to self-sufficiency <u>could</u> occur.

We have recorded instances of "clans" caught in the midst of a Kariera to Aranda transition who have had to leave their traditional marriage partners and in fact look elsewhere. Falkenberg, in <u>Kin and Totem</u>, records one amongst the Murinbata people of the Port Keats region of Western Australia:

> Among the Mari'djabin-Mari'djadi and Mari'ngar'-Magati-ge a man can belong to the same local clan as his mother-in-law and mother-in-law's brother. Among the Murin'bata, however, this is now considered wrong. At present the Murin'bata clearly tend to feel that <u>bip:inginar</u> (wife's mother) and <u>ile:nginar</u> (wife's mother's brother) should also come from 'a little bit far away' i.e. from another clan. This also applies to <u>kawu</u> (mother's mother's brother) . . . .

Such disagreements extend to "clans" <u>within</u> the same so-called 'tribe' of intermarrying "clans":

> This system (of two clan exchange), however, is not the norm for the whole Mari'ngar tribe. In some of the clans, as in the Der:ang'ar:a clan, one finds a number of deviations from this system.

The Der:ang'ar:a, in fact, distinguish two kinds of mother-in-law -- one who is in and one who is not in one's own "clan". Falkenberg goes on to report that this change from Kariera to

Aranda is proceeding in a north-south direction and that those in the middle, the Mari'ngar and Magati'ge, are beginning to turn away from their traditional marriage partners and are looking southward to the Murin'bata amongst whom the Aranda system has become more fully established.

The full implications of this transition will never be known. The mission station at Port Keats eventually attracted these and other peoples to make a much wider choice of marriage partners immediately available.

There is, however, another scenario in which one "clan" can become isolated from its associates having less to do with structural issues and more to do with the monist, locality-incorporative, tendencies that the structure in question has tamed. This is a "clan" bent on autonomy and self-determination in respect of its own resources and people when faced with ecological/demographic crisis. There is a known case amongst the Kaiadilt of Bentinck Island, south-west Queensland, as reported by Norman Tindale in 1962.

The Kaiadilt experienced severe drought on their island in the 1904s and when visited by Norman Tindale one <u>dolnoro</u> or "clan" was keeping a proportion of its women for marriage with its own members. The traditional system of the Kaiadilt was very close to that of the base-four Aranda. The "clan" seems to have been in the process of withdrawing into its relatively more abundant estate. However, closer examination of Tindale's data indicates that they were not yet so withdrawn that they married a person of the same personal totem within the "clan". A restricted definition of exogamy was still being followed. And the "clan" was still totemically linked to those of its company.

We have no way of knowing what the outcome would have been had the situation persisted. Fortunately the Islanders were subsequently removed to the mainland by the authorities to relieve their distress. Perhaps other "clans" too might have considered an independent course; perhaps the deviant "clan" would have been expelled -- or exterminated -- by its neighbours. On the other hand, perhaps rather than being greedy, the deviant "clan" was only following the dictates of a logic which concluded, 'withdraw and separate in the face of impending crisis'.

Whatever the scenario culminating in the isolation of the one, the consequence for its own future would be the same: it has relinquished the power to bend the other to itself in the absence of the will to do so. It has relinquished the institutions of peace. At best, it might end up with the Idea of abstract eternal jurisdiction in the singular intact, which for all practical purposes may be worse than no Idea at all. The world, after all, cannot accommodate more than one 'chosen people'.

It is interesting that the scenario I have painstakingly extracted from the early passages of Genesis -- monism, the emergence of pluralism, the fall back into monism, the possibility of redemption in pluralist terms -- is recorded much more explicitly in Aboriginal mythology and with a much happier ending.

The elder Strehlow, in Aranda-und Loritja-Stamme, records that according to Western Aranda tradition, humanity emerged in a shapeless mass of half-developed beings all grown together and undifferentiated. Mangarkunjerkunja, the Gecko, however, came down from the north to separate this mass into individual men and women and taught them the eight section system (four "clans" with two sections in each combining alternate generations into one category). But after he left the people fell into incestuous unions. Another culture hero, Katukankara, the Sandhill Wallaby, then came from the north to reinstitute the Law.

*   *   *   *   *

Genesis, then, myth or history? True or false? Or fiction that merely illustrates truth? These are going to be very difficult questions to answer even with locality-incorporation and kinline-confederation and the relation between them in mind. It is difficult enough when we take the text at face value, but a reading through theory prompts new facts to appear which were not heretofore obvious. For instance, we now understand why the evening and the morning are repeated through the first six days of Creation. They represent opposed complementarity and its apparent victory over opposition as such. They are the eternal constant in what appears a changing or unfolding universe. We now understand why there is no evening and morning on the seventh day: God has reflected on t(he)ir (another impliction of the reading) achievement and discovered a flaw -- life emerged out of a unity, a single element, the waters: In the beginning, then, was the fulfillment of opposition. Change not constancy is predominant.

Human activity in Genesis now clarifies itself as paradox-ical and ironic rather than contradictory and confused, as is the case without the theory in mind. We realize why it is Joseph's eldest brother, the one with the most to lose should his dreams come true, who in fact saves his life. Joseph is the agent of an experiment predestined to confirm the status quo. His life will change nothing. The direction of events takes on new and preg-nant meaning. The Israelites' move toward national unity at Babel is retrogressive, not progressive. The confounding of the languages and the dispersal of the people are a promise for the future, not a punishment for the past.

Now we grasp a sense in which Genesis could, in fact, be true. It is perhaps a portrayal of events and ideas through laws of history and laws of thought-about-history which are true. If real events and people were included in Genesis -- and no doubt they were -- it is because they were a product of forces felt but only dimly comprehended. In this sense we would, perhaps, be better to speak of Genesis as 'poetry' -- an emotive expression -- rather than 'myth' -- an intellectual expression -- strictly speaking.

The fact that Genesis is coded according to laws that are real might be what accounts for some remarkably good guesses about the unknowable, for instance, about the origins of life and the universe. Modern physics debates whether the world came into being with a quiet whimper or a big bang. Genesis shows how it could have been both -- a complementarity recoiling from syn-thesis. And does not biology tell us that life on earth emerged from the sea, moved onto the land and took to the air, leaving anomalous sea-air creatures -- like the great whales -- in its wake? Though how vegetation managed to emerge before the sun, as Northrop Frye points out, remains a mystery.

Of course, this is not the kind of thing most people are after when they ask about the Truth in the Bible. They want to know if the events, the people, the stories in fact happened. It is difficult to know.

The Israelites were, of course, an historical people. In the pre-Christian era they herded cattle and sheep and tended gardens in the land of Canaan in the Middle East. Today their descendants occupy the state of Israel, something less than the Canaan of old.

The old Canaan was a harsh land at the best of times. Permanent waterways were few and the main source of water was, in fact, the rain. When it failed to materialize there was drought and famine in the land. Human settlement, therefore, concentrated around wells and waterholes where people formed into tribes in an attempt to become self-sufficient and defend their territories against outsiders, that is, against people organized elsewhere in a similar fashion to themselves. Survival depended largely on force of numbers and an ability to hold territory, that is, on an effective military organization. This was accomplished by the institution of the chief and his hereditary continuity through his eldest son. Membership in the tribe itself, though, was determined through the female. Israelite folklore holds that this is for the very good reason that the mother alone knows the real identity of the father who also must be Israelite. As much as possible marriages were contained within the tribe but occasionally a chiefly line was forced to send a son or daughter outside to cement an alliance with a belligerent neighbour or one who would support them against a third force.

History also records that the land of Canaan stood in the path of the great powers of the time, lying as it did between Egypt to the southwest and Babylon to the north-east. Though of little value in and of itself, Canaan stood on one of the world's great trade and military routes linking Africa to Asia. Our theory suggest it is this circumstance which would have made the Israelites a force for good in the world. In fact, their movements and activities in the early historic period seem to have been informed by the anti-thesis ⟶ thesis ⟹ complementarity scenario.

About 3,500 years ago, Canaan and its peoples were ruled by the Egyptians. Then came the Hyksos, Semitic tribes from Syria -- descendants of the House of Shem in Biblical lore -- to overpower the Egyptians and assume control of Canaan. The Israelites' treck to Egypt in Joseph's time coincides with the period of Hyksos rule there. Being kindred people they would at least seem more likely allies than the Egyptians themselves. But then in the 16th century the Egyptians rose up and reconquered their homeland. The Israelites' situation there would now be precarious indeed. But the Mitanni, an Indo-European people to the north, moved to threaten the Egyptian cause. But then peace was negotiated with the Mitanni in the 15th century. Now the Israelites would be less useful and the Egyptians would move to hold them in check. Then in the 14th century yet another people, the Hittites, enter the scene to overpower the Mitanni and themselves threaten Egypt. Once again the Israelites would find themselves with some room to manoeuver and their own power would grow correspondingly. But then peace was once more struck and the Israelites would now pose an even greater threat to the internal security of Egypt. The suppression of Israel and the Exodus back to Canaan, in fact, occurs during this period.

The withdrawal syndrome evident here is also consistent with being caught in the "anti-thesis ⟶ thesis" trap of history -- the mythological response of a chosen people caught in an impossible situation with no one to turn to.

It is much more difficult, however, to locate the players in the act. The only evidence is the Bible itself. For instance, there is no record of Joseph in Egypt. None at all. Scholars who wish the Bible to be literally true in all respects set his rule during the Hyksos conquest. They explain that there is no record of his administration because the Egyptians would have eradicated all memory of the Hyksos period once they regained power. Sceptics point out that the events and customs associated with Joseph in the Bible, such as tax collecting, actually post-date the Hyksos occupation.

The same problem exists in relation to earlier episodes of Genesis. The places existed -- Ur, Babel, Sichem, for example -- but was there ever a flood? Did Abraham really sojourn in the land of Haran and enter into an alliance with a King, Abimalech, some time later? Did Jacob away to Padanaram to find a wife? The only evidence is the Bible itself.

There is archaeological evidence of floods in the Tigris-Euphrates river watershed, but one of such magnitude that all possibility of escape was precluded? Oddly enough there is evidence in the affirmative in Genesis itself, but perhaps not of a kind most Biblical scholars would accept.

The events of the flood follow a particular cycle: seven days from the building of the ark until the beginning of the rains, 40 days during which the waters rose, 150 days of flood, 40 days between the settling of the ark on Mount Ararat and the release of the dove, and seven days until the release of the second dove. Elsewhere in the world of myth we have found that such constant oscillation bespeaks natural forces beyond human control -- the comings and goings of the seasons, the rains, the sun and the moon, drought, flood.

On the other hand, our imagination is taxed less if we are asked to picture a man and his family with their livestock and belongings putting to sea in a ship to escape the evils of their modern world. We do know that in days of old the Persian Gulf extended inland to Ur, and Ur is where Abraham and his forbears, one of whom was Noah, are believed to have originated.

But surely, you might well say in this connection, we need only subtract the sequences of Genesis that decode according to the 'mythologics' of monism and pluralism in order to get a true picture of what really happened at the time. Surely these sequences are themselves untrue, the product of thought about history and society and sloppy thought at that!

The problem with this methodological dictate is that these thoughts, however imperfect, reach conclusions, however irrational (in the sense that they seek to escape coming to terms with problems that are real), and these conclusions translate into behaviour which can be put into practice. The Israelites, for instance, really did withdraw and separate from their enemies, create the illusion of solutions by establishing claims to land in absentia which no one else recognized.

To reiterate: people in monist history may fail to gain an adequate grasp of their true circumstances or simply deny their terms once they know them for what they really are. Instead they may seek to obfuscate their situation by proceeding analogically rather than analytically to handle the oppositions and contradictions that trouble their thoughts -- and their situation. They will substitute a pair of terms weaker than the original for the real ones in order to allow a mediator and find a 'solution'. In Noah, for example, the hard line previously drawn between the chosen few and unchosen many is temporarily blurred to allow representatives of both sides to come together in the context of the ark. The ark then contains them in apparent complementarity until a new beginning presumably begins.

But the containment is artificial, so too the beginning. It is merely a superficial enclosure exerting no permanent force on that which it contains. It leaves the sons of God and the daughters of men, humankind and animalkind, on the same unaltered course as before they entered the ark -- but with one difference. All parties now believe that a new course has been charted which will fundamentally alter their circumstances. Predictably, opposition, not really having been moderated or obliterated, re-emerges full-blown. It must for, as Lévi-Strauss points out in other contexts, it was real in life outside thought.

On the other hand, people caught on a pluralist side-track, particularly one for which they have no concepts, would proceed analytically rather than analogically in an effort to understand their circumstances. They would separate out their situation into its component parts in order to determine carefully its essential features. But in so doing they would see the weakeners removed which held apart heretofore unengaged oppositions, particularly since in this sidetrack it is opposition that informs their movement toward plurality. Once released, or revealed analogically through progressive strengthening rather than weakening, these oppositions threaten to become real and engulf them whole; thought rushes to separate them, isolate them, in the hopes of preventing an engagement. But alas, once the release is effected, real alternatives to the status quo are realized to exist. The temptation of Eve is a case in point: humankind is separated from God, man from woman, both from the Garden because of the initial appearance of a mediator.

(Comparing the two mythological processes we uncover an interesting paradox: in radical history mythological thought is conservative, in conservative history mythological thought is radical.)

Stories like the Tower of Babel, then, which code according to a mythological scenario could be evidence of a quality of thought with no practical implications. On the other hand, it could be that someone reflecting on the historical process of monism ordered its erection, someone reflecting on the subordinate force of pluralism, its abandonment.

(It is well to keep in mind that everyone everywhere is capable of both modes of mythological thought and that different historical courses, different circumstances and experiences, merely encourage one in us over the other.)

It is odd, but by drawing a clear distinction between myth and history and locating their respective laws of motion, I have only succeeded in drawing them even closer together.

* * * *

Where Genesis comes into its own as historical truth is in its account of life after the Fall -- in its outline of the locality-incorporative-based course that followed. Hunting and gathering, it declares, preceded agriculture. Cultivation, it goes on, preceded herding, preceded irrigation agriculture, preceded long-term planning. And, indeed, the anthropological evidence suggests that this was the case. The domestication of plants -- or at the least the systematic harvesting of grains found in nature -- seems to have originated some 13,000 years ago in the Middle East. The first domesticated animals were sheep, about 11,000 years ago, followed by goats, cattle and fowl. Anthropologists generally ascribe the order here to nature -- cultivated fields collected the crops and the crops collected the animals. The initial transformation from hunting and gathering to cultivation and herding, anthropologists usually ascribe to the problem of population size in relation to available resources. The new mode of production allows more people to make do with the same resources.

Genesis contains a more sophisticated account. In fact, people who space themselves in relatively small numbers over a relatively wide range of resources do face serious problems in time of crisis which could lead to technological change. With population rising and/or resources depleting they have but four choices -- move on to lands occupied by their neighbours after moving them off, form alliances, merge into larger wholes, or improve their techno-environmental efficiency. Since their neighbours are likely to be in the same circumstances as themselves, forming alliances is at best a temporary solution and merging is pointless. Conquest is difficult and costly but perhaps necessary. Technological change provides the best alternative but is difficult even at the worst of times. But occasionally it happens and moves at least a narrow segment of humankind along a kind of progress.

Genesis dwells on the difficulties imposed by society of actually implementing technological change and thereby achieving isolated self-sufficiency. This is the famous 'contradiction between the old social relations of production and the new technological means of production' located by Marx.

For reasons of continuity it is the first-born in Israelite society who inherits. But he represents, and continues, the less advanced technology -- the one practised in the previous generation. The innovators will be the later-born who don't share the first-born's sense of obligation to the past, including its technological achievements. But it is precisely these people who lack the political authority to implement their innovations. Were it not so, society would succumb in advance of the achievements, assuming they ever would materialize. How then to effect technological change without destroying the entire fabric of society? How not to and survive?

It is at least predictable that Genesis should dwell on this problem so intensely. As the Chosen People the Israelites suffered from self-imposed isolation more than most peoples. Cain and Abel, Esau and Jacob, Joseph and his brethren all faithfully record the actual dilemma: if the youngest succeeds, tried and tested true tradition suffers; if the eldest prevails, innovation is unlikely; where strict ability wins out, innovation is placed over tradition in social importance and the concept of the Chosen People is weakened. Exploiting the abilities of other cultures is an obvious way out of this latter dilemma -- leaving you, in the end, in the ascendancy -- but how to persuade your enemies to allow you in to do this? As Genesis so accurately illustrates, these problems are ever-present and irresolvable so long as you remain predominantly within the terms of monist history. The path out of this history lies in establishing abstract, eternal jurisdiction over territory by a diversity of people.

Doubtful. Within One lies death and destruction. Insofar as the suggestion implies a measure of self-sufficiency within the One, albeit with its Idea intact, it in fact constitutes a regression. Yet the alternative of one unself-sufficiency amongst self-sufficiencies would represent even more of a problem! At best human potential realized only within the Israelite nation leaving the technology-social relations of production problem to define everyone else's situation. The Israelites would avoid the problem themselves by drawing off the knowledge of other peoples so entrapped?

Their only real hope was, in fact, to locate another One in similar circumstances, likewise moved by anti-thesis into a complementary relations with themselves. What hope of this alone amongst Arab nations in the Middle East? Is it little wonder that the Israelites turned to God not only for practical guidance but also for further information on the matter?

As you will readily admit, when it comes to the question of Truth in Genesis, it's the Idea of God that's most difficult to accept. Beings alternately directing and misdirecting our existence? But this is precisely the point that should make one wonder. In Genesis God alone is uncodable as myth or history. T(he)y stand over and above thoughts and events, neither opposed nor complementary, both opposed and complementary, the source of events, thoughts, Creation.

And actually, in terms of our Codes, the existence of God is the easiest thing in the Bible to demonstrate. For to deny t(he)ir existence is merely to confirm it: anti-thesis ⟶ thesis. The code may be new but the idea is not. In fact, it was the gist of the argument put by St. Anselm of Cantebury a few years after the Norman Conquest of 1066 in his Proslogium.

To Anselm God must exist 'because he cannot be non-existent even in thought.' And, indeed, my theory implies that 'something' does in fact proceed from 'nothing'; to pose non-existence asserts existence. Or, as Anselm puts it in the context of 'God', "What are thou save the highest of all beings, alone self-existent, who has made all other things from nothing?" His 'argument', which runs something like this, in fact, codes according

to the theoretical formula at issue. Anselm put it in mock
dialogue with a Fool. Fool indeed who would deny the independent
existence of the other side of the argument standing there con-
fronting him:

anti-thesis ↓ thesis ↓ plurality	The Fool: Anselm: Anselm in relation to the Fool:	God does not exist; there is nothing greater than that which I can think. I am outside your thoughts: you hear and understand me; therefore there is some- thing greater than that which is in your thoughts. Since your thoughts about me and I myself both exist, there is clearly something greater than these that can be thought. What are thou, O Lord God, than whom nothing greater can be thought?

The transcendental implications notwithstanding, to my mind
God, like Dreamtime Beings, is the 'source' of Ideas with no
apparent material foundation. Indeed, it may be as simple as
that. Such Ideas do exist; the Idea of abstract, eternal, jurisdiction is, as I've said, one of them. 'Jurisdiction', unlike
the idea of a tree, a car, a person, has no object in reality
that can be observed, classified, compared and abstracted into a
concept. Some words are simply unfathomable.

We have now come full circle, back to a consideration of the
dialectic and its interpreters. The German philosopher Hegel
grasped the Idea as central to historical progress but set it
strictly on a thesis ⟶ anti-thesis ⟹ synthesis course. Its
purpose? Incorporation of lesser accomplishments. Its fulfillment? The monolithic German State. He did speak, though, of
'mediated unities' by which he meant that opposites, rather than
being dissolved in synthesis, might remain in suspended animation
once their power had been diminised by the process of unity.
Marx objected: ideas, he said, were but a reflection of material
reality, more often than not a distortion which masked its true

nature.   History, he also thought, moved according to the <u>thesis</u> ──➤ <u>anti-thesis</u> ══➤<u>synthesis</u> scenario, but the determining factor in its course was not Hegel's Idea, but a contradiction between the forces and relations of production which divided people into warring classes.   History, he thought, moved inexorably toward the emergence of the classless society -- really a society dominated by but one class, the workers, after they had incorporated or annihilated all the rest.

For Marx, the State (and lesser Ideas at earlier stages of evolution) were merely the means by which the ruling class of the day exerted its predominance.   It held no merit in itself, as perhaps it doesn't.   Private property, abstract personal jurisdiction over (in most cases) things, was an anathema to Marx too -- the root of all evil.   Even group property was reprehensible if the group in question formed part of the exploiting class.

What Marx failed to notice was that abstract jurisdiction, whether over citizens by (some) citizens in the State, or over things by individuals as property, might well end up as progressive developments if moved by forces of another order.   It was the nature of those forces that eluded Hegel too.

Marx perhaps erred in yet another aspect: his idea of what in fact constituted progress.   His social ideal was co-operation.   Here, as we have seen, it seems rather accommodation in interdependence that promises life for <u>all</u>.   In fact, we have linked co-operation to the monist scenario.

CO-OPERATE: "work together; concur in producing an effect." And, indeed, just what <u>is</u> the status of those with whom you do <u>not</u> co-operate?   Not only this, but I would hazard (another) guess that co-operation, in fact, marks the point of transition from defence to offence on the part of those who formerly separated and withdrew.   In other words, it marks the point at which they become like the very people who threaten them.   Is that progress?

An example might be Canada's contemporary native peoples as they combine to 'fight' for their rights.   And don't native leaders call on those they would lead to co-operate in forming a 'common front' against the society that has put up a common front against them for the past hundreds of years?

If co-operation was an obvious good for Marx, competition was an obvious evil and it too we have linked to the locality-incorporative/monist scenario. Competition poses a threat to those who can't, or won't, compete. And therein precisely lies its _progressive_ aspect: accommodation emerges in response. Not only then are there two sides to everything, but things are not always what they seem either.

In the final stages of history, thought Marx paralleling Hegel but on a material plane, the communes, no longer isolated pockets of co-operation (and, in my terms, warring factions), would once again reappear amongst us to be represented in the Assembly of the one-class worker State -- in the new national assembly. A noble ideal but there are really no theoretical grounds for this projection. It is rather that the very act of overthrow generates a 'plural' response in those overthrown -- as the totalitarian system established thereafter does in the generations that follow. In principle, much the same thing must occur in the course of ideological development as Hegel's many Ideas struggle into One.

Lévi-Strauss, for his part, developed the Marxist notion of idea as ideology to the point of demonstrating that much human thought was, indeed, an attempt to mask contradictions that were real, but through a cognitive process of weakening and substitution to create the illusion of solution. What he failed to see was the terms of an alternative logic. This was, I think, partly due to the fact that after studying in detail the social organization of the Australians and finding evidence of similar principles at work in South-east Asia, India and China (though not quite the principles located here), he then switched his interest to an anlysis of North and South American Indian mythology. There he found, as we would expect, the 'mythologic' of monism -- the predominant mode of thought of locality-incorporative peoples. For Lévi-Strauss, myth and social structure would

not articulate. And so he developed no general theory and instead went off in other directions into the recesses of the mind.

Even when treated in such a summary and simple manner -- or
perhaps because of it -- we gain a sense in which each of these
thinkers was right, and each wrong. Ideas are ideology but at
least one Idea is different: the Idea of abstract, eternal
jurisdiction. But it is the subdivision and recombination of
this Idea, not its ever expanding unity that constitutes its
significance. History does unfold according to the laws of the
Marxist (monist) materialistic dialectic, but only one stream,
one dimension, does so. We are continually being moved out of
this stream, this dimension, by the very laws of its own existence -- but only temporarily. The image that comes to mind is
that of the fabulous Phoenix, born in the ashes of its own destruction, dying in the flames of its own creation.

Hegel, Marx and Lévi-Strauss, then, would seem to have much
in common despite their apparent differences. All three were
theorists of monist history, the monist dimension in life; all
three held their theories to have universal validity -- monism
admits but one; all three failed to break through the monist
barrier; all three were Europeans. Can there be any doubt as to
its predominant mode of operation?:

> The Proletariat goes through various stages of
> development. With its birth begins its struggle
> with the bourgeoisie. At first the contest is car-
> ried on by individual labourers, then by the work
> people of a factory, then by the operatives of one
> trade, in one locality, against the individual
> bourgeois who directly exploit them.
>
> At this stage the labourers still form an incoher-
> ent mass scattered over the whole country, and
> broken up by their mutual competition. If anywhere
> they unite to form more compact bodies, this is not
> yet the consequence of their own active union, but
> of the union of the bourgeoisie, which class, in
> order to attain its own political ends, is compel-
> led to set the whole proletariat in motion, and is

moreover yet, for a time, able to do so . . . .
But with the development of industry the proletariat not only increases in number; it becomes concentrated in greater masses, its strength grows, and
it feels that strength more. The various interests
and conditions of life within the ranks of the
proletariat are more and more equalised, in proportion as machinery obliterates all distinctions of
labour, and nearly everywhere reduces wages to the
same low level. The growing competition among the
bourgeois, and the resulting commercial crises,
make the wages of the workers ever more fluctu-
ating. The unceasing improvement of machinery,
ever more rapidly developing, makes their liveli-
hood more and more precarious; the collisions between individual workmen and individual bourgeois
take more and more the character of collusions
between two classes. Thereupon the workers begin
to form combinations (trade unions) against the
bourgeois; they club together in order to keep up
the rate of wages; they found permanent associ-
ations in order to make provision beforehand for
these occasional revolts. Here and there the con-
test breaks out into riots.

(Manifesto of the Communist Party, 1848)

But then this is the subject of other deliberations. Here,
let me rather leave the reader with this idea, this image: Life
itself is two interwoven strands of matter, one the mirror image
of the other, linked without merging, growing only to arrive at a
fixed position:

D.N.A.: complementarity. So too our anatomical proportions: as Da Vinci observed, a balance of line and circle, line, the cross -- peace -- in the forefront. So too the female person: the two within the one who are two, indivisible and un-unifiable.

> 2:16 And the LORD God commanded the <u>man</u>, saying, Of every tree of the garden thou mayest freely eat:

> :17 But of the tree of knowledge of good and evil, thou shalt not eat of it:

Emphasis mine.

Selected Bibliography

St. Anselm. 1962. Basic Writings (trans. S.N. Deane). La
    Salle: Open Court.

Berndt, R.M. and C.H. 1945. Preliminary Report on Field Work in
    Western South Australia, Oceania, XIV no. 2, pp. 149-158.

_____, 1976. The World of the First Australians. Sydney:
    Ure Smith.

Bolle, Kees. 1980. The History of Religion and Anthropology,
    Epoché, vol. 7, nos. 1-2.

Bouissac, Paul. 1976. Circus and Culture. Bloomington: Indi-
    ana University Press.

Burridge, Kenelm. 1973. Encountering Aborigines. New York:
    Pergamon Press.

de Josselin de Jong, P.E., ed. 1977. Structural Anthropology in
    the Netherlands. The Hague: Martimus Nijhoff.

Dunning, R.W. 1959. Social and Economic Change Among the North-
    ern Ojibwa. Toronto: University of Toronto Press.

Fairweather, Eugene. 1956. A Scholastic Miscellany: Anselm to
    Ockham. Philadelphia: Westminster Press.

Falkenberg, Johannes. 1962. Kin and Totem. Oslo/New York:
    Oslo University Press.

Feit, Harvey. 1983. Algonkian Hunting Territories Before Con-
    tact. Paper prepared for the 3rd International Conference
    on Hunter-gatherers, Bad Homburg, West Germany, June.

Frye, Northrop. 1982. The Great Code. New York: Academic
    Press.

Harris, Marvin. 1971. Culture, Man and Nature. New York:
    Thomas Y. Crowell.

Hegel, George Wilhelm. 1967. Phenomenology of Mind (trans.
    J.B. Baille). New York: Harper and Row.

Holm, Bill. 1965. Northwest Coast Indian Art. Seattle: Uni-
    versity of Washington Press.

Jacobi, Jolande, ed. 1959. Complex, Archetype and Symbol in the Psychology of C.G. Jung. Princeton: University of Princeton Press.

Keller, Werner. 1982. The Bible as History. New York: Bantam.

Krader, Lawrence, ed. 1972. The Ethnological Notebooks of Karl Marx. Assen: Van Gorcum.

Lanoue, Guy. 1982. "Continuity and Change: the development of Political Self-definition among the Sekani of Northern British Columbia". (Ph.D. thesis, University of Toronto.)

Leach, Edmond. 1969. Genesis as Myth and other Essays. London: Jonathan Cape.

Lévi-Strauss, Claude. 1962. Totemism. London: Merlin Press.

_____, 1968. The Structural Study of Myth. In Structural Anthropology (trans. Jacobson and Schoepf). London: Allen Lane and Penguin Press.

_____, 1969. The Elementary Structures of Kinship (tran. Bell and von Sturmer, Rodney Needham ed.). London: Eyre and Spottiswoode.

Levitt, Dulcie. 1981. Plants and People: aboriginal uses of plants on Groote Eylandt. Canberra: Australian Institute of Aboriginal Studies.

MacKnight, Campbell. 1972. Macassans and Aborigines, Oceania 42, no. 4: 283-321.

Maddock, Kenneth. 1972. The Australian Aborigines. London: Allen Lane the Penguin Press.

Marx, Karl. 1848. Manifesto of the Communist Party.

_____, 1967. Capital: a critique of political economy. New York: International Publishers.

Mauss, Marcel. 1969. The Gift. London: Routledge and Kegan Paul.

May, Herbert, ed. 1974 (2nd edition). Oxford Bible Atlas. London: Oxford University Press.

Morgan, Lewis Henry. 1901/54. League of the Ho-De-No Sau-Nee or Iroquois. Vol. 1. New Haven: Human Area Relations File.

Needham, Rodney. 1962. Structure and Sentiment. Chicago: University of Chicago Press.

_____, 1980. Reconnaissances. Toronto: University of Toronto Press.

Oberg, Kalervo. 1973. The Social Economy of the Tlingit Indians. Vancouver: J.J. Douglas.

Parkman, Francis. 1885. The Jesuits of North America. London: Macmillan.

Plant, Raymond. 1983. Hegel. Oxford: Blackwell.

Potok, Chaim. 1978. Wanderings. New York: Fawcett-Crest.

Pratt, E.J. 1940. Brébeuf and his Bretheren. Toronto: Macmillan.

Pretty, G.L. 1976. The Excavations at Roonka Flat, South Australia: an insight into ancient South Australian society. Adelaide: South Australian Museum.

Rose, F.G.G. Classification of Kin, Age Structure and Marriage Amongst the Groote Eylandt Aborigines. Berlin: Academie Verlag.

Rosman, A., and P.G. Rubel. 1971. Feasting with Mine Enemy. New York: Columbia University Press.

Rousseau, Jerome. 1979. Stratification and Chiefship: a comparison of Kwakiutl and Kayan, In Challenging Anthropology (G.A. Smith and D.H. Turner eds.). Toronto: McGraw-Hill Ryerson.

Ryan, Michael. 1982. Marxism and Deconstruction. Baltimore: John Hopkins University Press.

Sahlins, Marshall. 1976. Culture and Practical Reason. Chicago: University of Chicago Press.

Skinner, Alanson. 1911. Notes on Eastern Cree and Northern Saulteaux. American Museum of Natural History, Vol. IX, pt. 1.

Speck, F.G. 1914. The Double-Curve Motif in Northeastern Algonkian Art. Canada: Department of Mines Geological Survey, Memoir 42.

Spencer, B. and F.J. Gillen. 1927. The Arunta: a study of a stone age people. London: Macmillan.

Stevens, James R. and Carl Ray. 1971. Sacred Legends of the Sandy Lake Cree. Toronto: McClelland and Stewart.

Strehlow, C. 1907-20. Aranda-und Loritja-Stamme, in Zentral-Australien. Frankfurt: Veroffentlichungen des Frankfurter Museums fur Volkerkunde.

Strehlow, T.G.H. 1947. Aranda Traditions. Melbourne: Melbourne University Press.

_____, 1968. Journey to Horseshoe Bend. Sydney: Rigby.

_____, 1971. Songs of Central Australia. Sydney: Angus and Robertson.

Swanton, John R. 1909. Tlingit Myths and Texts. Bureau of American Ethnology, Bulletin 39. Washington.

Swartz, Marc J. and David K. Jordan. 1976. Anthropology. New York: John Wiley and Sons.

Tanner, Adrian. 1979. Bringing Home Animals. London: C. Hurst.

Tindale, Norman B. 1936. Legend of the Wati Kutjara, Warbuton Range, Western Australia, Oceania. Vol. 7, No. 2, pp. 169-185.

_____, 1962. Some Population Changes among the Kaiadilt of Bentinck Island, Queensland. Records of the South Australian Museum, 14: 297-336.

_____, 1974. Aboriginal Tribes of Australia. Berkeley: University of California Press.

Turner, David H. 1974. Tradition and Transformation: a study of Aborigines in the Groote Eylandt area, northern Australia. Canberra: Australian Institute of Aboriginal Studies.

_____, 1977. Shamattawa: the structure of social relations in a northern Algonkian band. Ottawa: National Museums of Man (with P. Wertman).

_____, 1977. Windigo Mythology and the Analysis of Cree Social Structure, Anthropologica, Vol. XIX, no. 1, pp. 63-73.

_____, 1978a. <u>Dialectics in Tradition: myth and social structure in two hunter-gatherer societies</u>. Occasional Paper 36 of the Royal Anthropological Institute, London.

_____, 1978b. Ideology and Elementary Structures, <u>Anthropologica</u>, Vol. XX, nos 1-2, pp. 223-247.

_____, 1980a. <u>Australian Aboriginal Social Organization</u>. New York/Canberra: Humanities Press/Australian Institute of Aboriginal Studies.

_____, 1980b. Les Aborigènes Australiens, s'adaptent surtant à la mode. <u>Anthropologie et Sociétés</u>, Vol. 4, no. 3, pp. 3-27, 1980.

_____, 1985. The Warnindilyaugwa Relationship System: a computer simulation. In <u>New Trends in Mathematical Anthropology</u> (Gisèle de Meur ed.). London: Routledge.

von Brandenstein, C.G. 1982. <u>Names and Substance of the Australian Section System</u>. Chicago: University of Chicago Press.

Warner, Lloyd. 1958. <u>A Black Civilization</u>. New York: Harper Torchbook.

Worsley, P.M. 1954. The Changing Social Structure of the Warnindilyaugwa (Ph.D. thesis, The Australian National University).

_____, 1979. One World or Three? <u>Proceedings</u>, Berlin: Institut fur Vergleichende Sozialforschung.

Herbert W. Basser

MIDRASHIC INTERPRETATIONS
OF THE SONG OF MOSES

American University Studies: Series VII, Theology and Religion. Vol. 2
ISBN 0-8204-0065-3   326 pp.   pb./lam., US $ 28.85
recommended prices – alterations reserved

This work provides a translation of, and a commentary to the text of *Sifre Ha'azinu*. Finkelstein's edition (1939, reprinted JTS 1969) and selected readings of the London manuscript of this midrash appear in translation with full notes covering textual observations, philological inquiries and exegetical problems. The following ideas are discussed within the course of the work: midrashic forms, the use of Scripture in midrash, the dating of the traditions and of the recording of this midrash, the use of apologetic and polemic in midrash. An *Introduction* and *Conclusion* have been provided which discuss the items in this midrash which are relevant to the academic study of Judaism. The literary aspects of this midrash on Deut. 32 are used to exemplify *midrashim* on poetic Scriptures.

Contents: Introduction discussing literary, theological, historical aspects of midrash – Translation and analysis of the midrash to Deut. 32. Sifre Deuteronomy – Conclusion summing up the findings in the work.

PETER LANG PUBLISHING, INC.
34 East 39th Street
USA – New York, NY 10016